Unmasking the Social Engineer

The Human Element of Security

Christopher Hadnagy
Dr. Paul Ekman

D1248878

WILEY

Unmasking the Social Engineer: The Human Element of Security

Published by
John Wiley & Sons, Inc.
10475 Crosspoint Boulevard
Indianapolis, IN 46256
www.wiley.com

Copyright ©2014 by John Wiley & Sons, Inc., Indianapolis, Indiana

Published simultaneously in Canada

ISBN: 978-1-118-60857-9
ISBN: 978-1-118-60865-4 (ebk)
ISBN: 978-1-118-89956-4 (ebk)

Manufactured in the United States of America

10 9 8 7 6 5 4 3 2 1

For general information on our other products and services please contact our Customer Care Department within the United States at (877) 762-2974, outside the United States at (317) 572-3993 or fax (317) 572-4002.

Wiley publishes in a variety of print and electronic formats and by print-on-demand. Some material included with standard print versions of this book may not be included in e-books or in print-on-demand. If this book refers to media such as a CD or DVD that is not included in the version you purchased, you may download this material at http://booksupport.wiley.com. For more information about Wiley products, visit www.wiley.com.

Library of Congress Control Number: 2013954093

To my beautiful wife, Areesa, who is my only true love.

To my son, Colin, for being one of the most reasonable, smart, and amazing people I have ever met.

To my precious little daughter, Amaya, who is the reason my heart is overflowing with positive emotions.

To Dr. Paul Ekman whose work, friendship, and help made this book possible.

About the Author

Chris **Hadnagy**, aka loganWHD, is the President and Chief Human Hacker of Social-Engineer, Inc. He specializes in understanding the ways in which malicious attackers are able to exploit human weaknesses to obtain access to information and resources through manipulation and deceit. He has been in security and technology for over 16 years.

Chris is a graduate of Dr. Paul Ekman's courses in microexpressions, having passed the certification requirements with an Expert Level grade. He also has significant experience in training and educating students in nonverbal communications. He also holds certifications as an Offensive Security Certified Professional (OSCP) and an Offensive Security Wireless Professional (OSWP).

Chris has written a number of articles for local, national, and international publications and journals including *PenTest* magazine, EthicalHacker.net, and local and national business journals. In addition, he is the author of the best-selling book, *Social Engineering: The Art of Human Hacking* (Wiley, 2011).

Chris has also developed one of the web's most successful security podcasts. The monthly Social-Engineer.org podcast spends time analyzing an individual who must use influence and persuasion in his or her daily life. By dissecting their choices and actions, we can learn to enhance our abilities. That same analysis applies to the equally popular SEORG newsletter. Over the years, both the podcast and the newsletter have become a staple in most serious security practices and are used by Fortune 500 companies around the world to educate their staff.

Finally, Chris has launched a line of professional social engineering training and penetration testing services at Social-Engineer.com. His goal is to assist companies in remaining secure by educating them on the methods used by malicious attackers. He accomplishes this by analyzing, studying, dissecting, and then performing the very same attacks used during some of the most recent breaches of corporate security (such as Sony, HB Gary, Lockheed Martin, and more). Chris is able to help companies understand their vulnerabilities, mitigate issues, and maintain appropriate levels of education and security.

About the Technical Editor

Paul Kelly has been with the Paul Ekman Group (PEG) since 2005, and currently serves as Dr. Ekman's Director for Law Enforcement and Security Workshops within North America. As such, he coordinates PEG workshops for U.S. military commands, U.S. intelligence agencies, national security organizations, and federal, state, and local police departments.

After graduating from Brown University with a B.A. in Political Science, Paul received a commission as an officer in the U.S. Marine Corps. A decorated Vietnam veteran, he served with the 3rd Force Recon Co. and also with MACV. His military training included the U.S. Army's Interrogation, PSYOP, and Civil Affairs/Military Government Schools, and the USMC Command and Staff College. He attained the rank of Major, USMCR.

After receiving his M.A. in Asian Studies from the University of Hawaii, where he studied Chinese Mandarin, Paul served for over 20 years as a special agent in the U.S. Secret Service (USSS) in a variety of protective, investigative, intelligence, and training assignments. As an instructor in the USSS, he taught interviewing techniques, technical security, and assailant methodology. During that time, he also served on the adjunct faculty of the National Security Agency (NSA), teaching OPSEC at their National Cryptologic School while concurrently working in the USSS OPSEC/Risk Management and Emergency Preparedness Programs. He retired as Assistant Special Agent in Charge of the White House Division.

After his retirement from the Secret Service, Paul was a Course Director for the Department of State's International Law Enforcement Academy in Budapest, Hungary, and an Instructor for the State Department's Anti-Terrorism Assistance Program. His travels have taken him all over the world, including Afghanistan, Bosnia, China, Egypt, Germany, Hungary,

India, Israel, Japan, Jordan, Korea, and Pakistan He also was a security consultant for several Olympic Games, the Mediterranean Games, the University Games, and the World Cup.

He met Dr. Ekman after hearing a presentation on facial microexpressions, or "micros," and learning that they were both involuntary and cross-cultural/universal. A very interesting facet of Paul's communication skills is having been identified as a "Truth Wizard" from Dr. Ekman's research with Dr. Maureen O'Sullivan on assessing credibility and detecting deception. These "Wizards," approximately 50 in number, constitute the top one-third of one percent (99.666 percentile) of more than 15,000 people surveyed and have demonstrated a significantly higher accuracy rate (80 percent threshold) than the average (53 percent). PK and I have been in frequent contact over the years regarding nonverbals, and especially micros; much of his advice and experience is found on the pages of this book, and especially in Chapter 5, "The Science Behind the Face."

Paul is a member of the International Association of Chiefs of Police (IACP) and ASIS International; other professional affiliations have included the OPSEC Professionals' Society, the International Association of Financial Crimes Investigators, the International Organization of Asian Crime Investigators & Specialists, and the International Association of Bomb Technicians and Investigators. He also serves as Chairman Emeritus of the Board of Trustees for the Massachusetts Maritime Academy.

Credits

Executive Editor
Carol Long

Project Editor
Brian Herrmann

Technical Editor
Paul Kelly

Production Editor
Christine Mugnolo

Copy Editor
Gayle Johnson

Editorial Manager
Mary Beth Wakefield

Freelancer Editorial Manager
Rosemarie Graham

Associate Director of Marketing
David Mayhew

Marketing Manager
Ashley Zurcher

Business Manager
Amy Knies

Vice President and Executive Group Publisher
Richard Swadley

Associate Publisher
Jim Minatel

Project Coordinator, Cover
Katie Crocker

Proofreader
Nancy Carrasco

Indexer
Robert Swanson

Cover Image
©iStockphoto.com/artcasta

Cover Designer
Ryan Sneed

Contents

II Decoding the Language of the Body 51

3 Understanding the Language of the Hands 53

4 The Torso, Legs, and Feet. 81

5 The Science Behind the Face 99

Foreword

From my initial research into reading the emotions of the face, to my more recent collaboration with the Dalai Lama in writing *Emotional Awareness: Overcoming the Obstacles to Psychological Balance and Compassion* (Holt Paperbacks, 2009), understanding people and their interactions with others has been my passion. I have spent decades examining not only how emotion is displayed, but also what people do and do not understand about why their emotions are triggered and how they behave once they become emotional. Doing so has enlarged my perspective on how to improve emotional life.

A little over four years ago, Chris reached out to me with his idea of blending my life's work with his research related to social engineering. It was very interesting to listen to him talk about his work. He made people aware of the manipulative efforts of certain people to exploit them, and he showed them how to reduce their personal and/or corporate vulnerability to such efforts. The goal of combining our work to help mitigate this risk was the key factor in my choosing to support Chris in the writing of this book.

Chris has nearly embarrassed me with his praise for my work and his interest in it. However, there is a benefit! He has worked hard to make my work known and, more importantly, useful to those working in social engineering. He also has been very responsive to the feedback I have given him and to the input provided by PEG trainer Paul Kelly, his technical editor. PK invested a great deal of time in reviewing this book, making suggestions and providing relevant examples of his own, drawn from his extraordinary experience in the fields of intelligence and national security.

Specifically, in reading Chapter 5 on facial expressions, and the section in Chapter 8 on conversational signals, you have the benefit of my work, PK's experience and insight, and Chris's knowledge of social engineering—an exciting, unique, and, I hope, rewarding blend.

Enjoy this book. Use its information and the decades of research that have been used to compile it to keep yourself, your family, your coworkers, and your business more secure.

Paul Ekman, PhD
Professor of psychology
emeritus, UCSF

President, Paul Ekman
Group LLC (PEG)
November 2013

Acknowledgments and Preface

As I planned this book, many people inspired me and helped me along the way. First and foremost is my family.

My wife, Areesa: You are the most patient person I know. The deeper I get into writing, the more reclusive I become. You have supported me, encouraged me, and made this life possible. Not many women can deal with being married to a professional social engineer. Answering phone calls using a different name and speaking with people who believe I am someone else. Having fake social media profiles online. Traveling the globe breaking into places and teaching others how to do the same. You are a remarkably patient, kind, and beautiful person. I am truly honored to have you as my wife. The first 20 years have been amazing. Let's make the next 20 even better! I love you.

My son, Colin: I've never met anyone who loves to read and learn like you do. If I mention a topic during family time, you later read about it and then can talk about it intelligently. When I took you through the five-day course, I didn't know what to expect, or if you would like it. It was great to watch you grow and expand your horizons. I believe that you will do amazing things in your life, and that your happy, easygoing personality will make you a real success. I love you, buddy.

My daughter, Amaya: You are the reason behind my smile. I look at you, and my world lights up. I love you so much. I remember when you were little, you would sit on my shoulders while I worked, sometimes for hours. Recently you passed the Ekman training with an 89 percent! You inspire me to be a better person. Your unconditional love and support are an inspiration. Your joy for life, your smile, and your amazing personality are some of the things I cherish most in my life. I love you with all my heart. You've made me a better person, father, and human being.

Many other people inspired and encouraged me. Brad "the Nurse" Smith, one of the most inspirational people I ever met.

Nick Furneaux: I feel like I have known you my whole life, like we were brothers separated at birth. Your encouragement during this process really helped me—not just with this book, but with my life. You and your family have been a gift to my family. You really are like a brother to me.

Ben and Selena Barnes: You know I love you. You are truly the face of this book, because your pictures grace the pages. Your patience while I made you contort your faces and bodies made this book even better. How great it has been to get to know you and have you as part of our family.

The last year and a half I have grown a great team with my company, Social-Engineer, Inc. Amanda: Even though I have known you since you were a tiny little nothing, and I fire you about 50 times a day, and I stress you out by doing things that drive OCD people crazy, and you have to hear "I'm Batman!" about 400 times a day, you are great. You really helped me focus, taking care of things when I had to go "off the grid" for a bit to write. Just please don't try to clean my office.

Michele: Who would have thought one conversation with Ping (love ya, Ping) would change our lives forever? Thanks to her recommendation, this year has been amazing. I can't thank you enough for helping me with research, kicking me into gear often, keeping me grounded, and just being a source of solid support as we grow. I hope this is the start of a long relationship as we build Social-Engineer into an even more amazing company. As you said to me in one of my most stressed times, "There's always hope."

Robin Dreeke: One of my favorite "I's" in the world. Who would have thought that when we met a few years ago it would turn into all this? You are a lot of fun to train with, and you have become a close friend. Thank you for all the great conversations and letting me bounce my ideas off you.

My thank-yous would be incomplete if I didn't thank the InfoSec community, which contains some of the most open-minded and amazing people I have ever met. Your encouragement to keep going and expand my knowledge helped me consider writing a second book. Thank you for the great feedback, the love, and even the occasional criticism. Thanks for all the hugs, too (except you, Dave; you can keep the hugs).

The introduction explains in detail how I came to work with Dr. Paul Ekman and Paul Kelly. I just want to offer a wholehearted thank-you here. PK, when we met, I didn't know if you would like me. You are one of the original microexpression wizards. You worked with Ekman for years and have a long history of working with the federal government, solving crimes, and protecting people. I am just a human hacker, but you had such an open mind for discussing how our paths crossed and how we could work together. Thank you, PK. You have come to be a close friend and a great source of advice and encouragement. Thank you.

Dr. Ekman, I'm not sure why you made that return call to me a few years ago. I'm not sure why you spent those hours on the phone with me, and why you let me sit with you in your home, talking about the future of social engineering and nonverbal communications. I may never know why, but whatever the reasons, thank you, thank you, thank you! Your firm direction and the kindness you showed me impacted my life and my direction. Your research and life's work were why I could spend time using, learning about, and then writing about social engineering in my industry. Paul, you are a great man and a wonderful mentor. Thank you.

Each person listed here has affected my life and helped this book come into existence. Thank you for your help in making this happen.

I remember how I felt when I began writing my first book. I just wanted to share my experiences and what I had learned along the path of who I had become. More than two years later, I sat down with a much more defined vision of what I wanted to accomplish in my second book. I knew I didn't want a 300-page rant that was just my opinions. If I were to write another book, I wanted it to be something that would be based on science. But I started to wonder, "Who am I? Why would anyone want to read a book about science by a social engineer?"

Then I attended a conference with my good friend Brad Smith. As we discussed this topic, he smiled warmly, touched my arm, and said to me with confidence, "Chris, you weren't born with these skills. Your path, your struggles, what you did to become who you are—these are life lessons that anyone with interest in this field would cherish."

A year later Brad passed away, but his words stuck with me. I began thinking about my journey of running a social engineering firm, having employees, teaching a five-day class and services all centered around my skills. I started to think about the skills that had the biggest effect on me, and nonverbal communication was the one that changed how I communicate.

I hope you enjoy reading this book. I hope you keep an open mind and try a few of the techniques described here to prove to yourself that they work. This book represents a new chapter in my life—another chance to pour out my soul and share some of the things I've learned along my journey.

I'm sure this book won't please everyone. I'm sure you will find some errors. But I hope I was successful at taking the comments, ideas, criticisms, and reviews from my first book and making this one much better.

Thank you for letting me into your mind for a while.

Christopher Hadnagy
October 2013

Introduction

I have taught myself to notice what I see.

—*Sherlock Holmes*

When I decided to write another book, I needed to spend some time thinking about the topic I wanted to cover. My *Social Engineering: The Art of Human Hacking* (Wiley, 2011) was one of the first books to walk the reader through all the skills that comprise an expert social engineer. These skills are flat, though, because you practice them and master them—there are no advanced topics.

Social Engineering is a simple and basic book that outlines what social engineering is and what I feel it takes to develop and use social engineering skills in your daily life. In addition, as many of my readers have noticed, I had to adjust my understanding, thinking, and training to come more in line with proven scientific facts.

As I thought about what excited me about social engineering and what skills I found helped me the most, I started to reflect on the journey I had taken over the last few years.

I've always found the psychology and physiology of human interaction fascinating. Although I do not have a degree in either field, I believe understanding these aspects of communication can enhance your ability to understand, interpret, and utilize skills related to these aspects in everyday communications.

As I began my research, I headed to a bookstore and bought books on particular topics that piqued my interest. This is when I first saw the books *Emotions Revealed* and *Unmasking the Face* by Dr. Paul Ekman.

I bought them and couldn't put them down. This was before Dr. Ekman had a website with interactive training courses. I was determined to locate and speak with him.

As I began to read *Emotions Revealed* I began to understand things that I had been subconsciously registering for years—things like when facial expressions didn't match verbal content and expressions for emotions that were trying to be hidden. The topic fascinated me, so I started to read all I could on body language and facial expressions. After reading these books and practicing as much as I could with their photographs, I found a website selling Dr. Ekman's Facial Action Coding System (FACS) course. The FACS course picks apart every muscle in the face and describes how it is triggered, what it controls, and what it looks like when used. I quickly bought that course and found out it was a treasure trove of information, but not for the faint of heart.

At this time, I was working on developing a course that would help security professionals learn the arts and sciences involved in social engineering. The course became a five-day foundational training program that would help teach enough of the skills to give the students a head start. At this point in my life, I decided to do something that would change my life forever.

I decided that it was time. I couldn't contain myself any longer; I had to speak to Dr. Ekman. It took me a while to find Dr. Ekman's email address and phone number, but eventually he and I talked on the phone.

To this day I cannot tell you why he spent so much time answering my questions and telling me about his research. I do know the time he gave me had a massive impact on my life, because Dr. Ekman and I developed a friendship. Over two years later I found myself sitting in his home, talking about the future of social engineering research involving the use of nonverbal communication.

After I launched my course, Dr. Ekman reviewed my materials and helped me perfect how I taught the section on nonverbal communication. He also helped me see how important this topic is when reading and dealing with other people. Not just the face, but also the whole body offers important cues for understanding what someone is truly saying during communication.

I'm telling you this story because it's what led me to write this book. My friendship with, and respect for, Dr. Ekman, my study of nonverbal communication, and my using those skills in my social engineering practice over the last few years helped me decide to call this book *Unmasking the Social Engineer*.

Each part of your body tells a story about your emotions. Each piece, when combined with the others, can help you understand what someone is feeling and saying when he or she communicates with you or is trying to hide from you.

Why should you care about this topic? Suppose that, while communicating with your spouse, kids, boss, coworkers, and others, you could decipher signs of discomfort. Suppose you could tell whether they were feeling happiness, sadness, anger, fear, or other emotions they didn't want you to see. Suppose that, when asking for a raise, you could see that your boss has some doubts. How would any of this affect your ability to adapt, adjust, and enhance your communication style? Now consider a social engineering engagement. When you are speaking to your target, what would it do for you to see that he is feeling anger, sadness, fear, or happiness? If you could look across the room at two people talking and see that one is feeling uncomfortable, could this fact assist you in your approach?

Being able not only to see but to decipher these signs will enhance your communication skills, and that is the primary reason to read this book. Secondarily, this book will enhance the skills of any social engineering professional to get the most out of their engagements with others.

We have all listened to a "gut feeling" when dealing with others. Sometimes you instantly like or dislike a person, for example. Sometimes gut feelings arise without any or very little actual communication. Have you ever wondered why this is the case?

A lot of what you base your gut feelings on involves how someone communicates nonverbally. Your brain picks up on these cues and then triggers an emotional response that creates a certain depth of feeling toward that person. Learning how to turn on this talent and use it to your benefit will give you power during any communication that you will quickly grow to enjoy.

From writing my first book, I learned that I can't please everyone. You might disagree with certain points in this book. That is fine and I encourage and look forward to open communication about these topics from you, the reader.

Feel free to reach out to me about these things. I am always open to constructive criticism. My website is www.social-engineer.com. There you will find ways to communicate with me.

Also, I do not claim that this book is based on new research that has never been released. As a matter of fact, this book is largely based on the research and work of some of the greatest minds of our time. The reason this book is different is because, until now, no book has compiled all this research for social engineers. No book has shown you how to use these skills as a social engineer. No book has been written by a social engineer and edited, proofed, and checked for scientific accuracy by two of the greatest men in this field— Dr. Paul Ekman and Paul Kelly.

One of the questions I get asked so often is how I developed my relationship with Dr. Ekman. Let me take a few moments to answer this question in this introduction.

The Scholar and the Student

One of my fears in initially trying to reach out to Dr. Ekman was that he was a world-renowned scientist and researcher, known for pioneering a whole area of study and research. Me...well, I am just a guy who really knows how to talk to people and enjoys "hacking things." I began to ask why he would want to spend his valuable time with me.

I first reached out to Dr. Ekman through his assistant and his website to invite him on my monthly Social-Engineer podcast. Truly surprised, Dr. Ekman asked to spend some time with me on the phone. We spent two hours talking that first day about my practice, what I did for work, and how it applied to his field.

Dr. Ekman may have been up in years, but he got the concepts of social engineering right away and saw applications for them. At that time he accepted my invitation to come on the podcast. We had one of our most downloaded podcasts ever with Dr. Ekman.

After that he reviewed the chapter of my five-day course related to nonverbals, helped me perfect my teaching method, and allowed me to use his Micro Expression Training Tool (METT) software in the course to help hone the students' skills during the day.

A few months later I found myself sitting on the balcony of Dr. Ekman's apartment talking about social engineering and microexpressions. It was then that I told him I wanted to write a book that took his decades of research and applied it to a field in which it had never been applied before.

But I told him I would only do it with his blessing and support. I would not take on this task without his help, training, editing, and correction. I am serious about making sure what is said in this book is backed by science, accuracy, and years of proof. About a year later, Dr. Ekman agreed to work with me and suggested that his longtime associate, Paul Kelly (or PK) would be a part of this process.

PK and I developed a friendship through this process that helped me to learn from one of Dr. Ekman's senior instructors. Dr. Ekman and PK spent a considerable amount of time with me to ensure that I understood the concepts and to help me make sure this book was scientifically accurate. Some of this collaboration is illustrated in Figures I-1 through I-4.

Figure I-1: Dr. Ekman and me reviewing some of the pictures for the book

Figure I-2: Dr. Ekman giving me some advice for proper facial expression usage for the book

Figure I-3: Dr. Ekman allowing me to explain my concept for using certain pictures

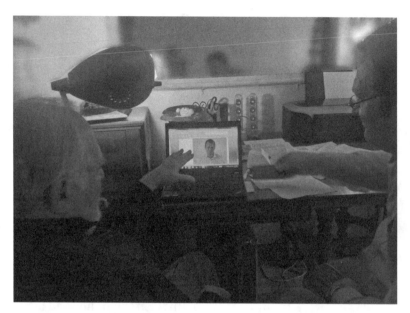

Figure I-4: Dr. Ekman helping me understand the deeper dimensions of some expressions

Despite all of this, one of the things that moved me even more is the time that Dr. Ekman gave my daughter, Amaya. My daughter took an interest in Dr. Ekman's work and took his online facial expression reading course, scoring an 89 percent. When she heard I was going to meet him in NYC, she begged me to let her come.

During that session, Amaya showed Dr. Ekman some of her work that was inspired by his daughter, Eve. She had made a collage of facial expressions imitating Eve from *Emotions Revealed*. Dr. Ekman took one look and said, "If you don't use this young lady in your book you are doing a disservice."

Figure I-5: Dr. Ekman working with Amaya to perfect her expressions

In the spirit of Eve Ekman from so many years ago, my daughter, Amaya, makes her debut in Chapter 5 of this book showing us her skill in mimicking facial expressions.

In the end, what I can say is that I am proud to have Paul Ekman and Paul Kelly supporting me in this book, as I know what I am writing is accurate and proven. Even more so, they have become my mentors and friends.

Let's quickly review the topics covered in this book.

Chapter 1 takes an in-depth look at nonverbal communication and how it works from a scientific point of view.

Chapter 2 describes what social engineering is and how it is used. This chapter discusses how several recent real-life attacks used social engineering and what you can learn from these incidents.

Chapter 3 considers the science of the hands, a subset of body language, describing how you can decipher emotions displayed through the use of the hands.

Chapter 4 analyzes the emotions revealed by other key aspects of body language—the torso, legs, and feet. What does it mean when someone points his or her feet toward the door? Are signs of comfort or discomfort hidden in how someone stands or leans? Being able to pick up on these cues will enhance your ability to read anyone fast.

Chapter 5 is chock-full of research, data, and facts about the human face. The science of the face is vital. The face is key to your emotions and is one of your biggest communication tools. Learning to understand, decipher, and use the face can make you seem like a mind reader.

Many people think that the science behind microexpressions (very brief, involuntary, and cross-cultural/universal facial expressions) is invalid and that no one can be taught to read facial expressions quickly. Chapter 5 is proof of the advancements in this science, led by Dr. Ekman, and how it is scientific fact. The vast majority of students improve this skill after as few as two hours of training, some significantly.

One of the greatest myths is that you can tell if someone is lying within seconds. That is untrue, but you *can* tell if someone is comfortable. Displaying signs of discomfort can reveal much about the person's state of mind and how it can be influenced. Chapter 6 focuses on how to look for and understand signs of discomfort.

Chapter 7 takes a small step away from the outside of the body and focuses on the brain, specifically the amygdala. This little portion of the brain that controls the nonverbal responses to emotional triggers will be discussed here. Also, this chapter answers the question of whether you can have your amygdala hijacked, and if so, how and to what effect.

Next we need to start applying this knowledge to the social engineering field, specifically elicitation, the heart of social engineering. Chapter 8 discusses how nonverbal communication affects the elicitation process.

Chapter 9 concludes the book with practical application as a security professional and answers the question, "How can this information be used to audit, educate, enhance, test, and protect yourself, your family, and your company?"

In this book, I convey what I know and how I have used this knowledge in my life as a social engineer. I have studied, researched, and talked with the world's experts about these topics. I have worked with them and gleaned knowledge from them to perfect my craft. Many people who have devoted their lives to understanding one or a few aspects of human communication have contributed to this book in some way.

My work with Robin Dreeke, Director of the FBI's Behavioral Analysis Unit and an expert on behavioral communication, has taught me a lot. I have learned how to read people's communication styles fast, how to build rapport with anyone quickly, and how to adjust my own style to be more appealing to others. He has truly changed my life.

On my Social-Engineer podcast, I interviewed great minds such as Dr. Ellen Langer, a Harvard psychologist who wrote a book on her theory of mindlessness, in which people go through their daily routines without thinking. Understanding this research affects how we look for and read signs of comfort or discomfort in those we are communicating with.

Paul Kelly has been an invaluable resource. His years with the US Secret Service as well as working with Dr. Ekman as a "natural" in reading microexpressions lend themselves to this book in helping to ensure that all I said was accurate. In addition, his friendship, support, and encouragement have been nothing but inspiring over these many months.

One of the most amazing conversations I ever had was with behavior economist Dan Ariely. His work and research on predictable irrationality have enhanced how we understand framing others and ourselves for complete change.

Kevin Hogan, a renowned expert on the psychology of persuasion, spent some time with me explaining how persuasion works and how his research can help us understand the power of making people do what you want.

I can't complete this Introduction without again mentioning Dr. Paul Ekman. Not only has he become a friend and mentor, but his books, training materials, and scientific research have changed how we understand communication. Dr. Ekman has taken a leap of faith in me and trusted me to take the "torch" of his life's work into a field that desperately needs it.

Using This Book as a Social Engineer

Voltaire is credited as being the first to say, "With great power comes great responsibility."

When I give my five-day training courses, I have been told that learning about social engineering is like being able to read minds. I don't teach people how to read minds. But you can learn how to communicate the way your target wants to be communicated with, read his or her subtle nonverbal cues, and display reinforcing nonverbals on your side. Doing so gives the person you are dealing with the feeling that communicating with you is in his or her best interest.

I hope you are reading this book with the intent of learning how to be a better communicator. Some studies like to attach numbers to how much of what we say is nonverbal. Dr. Ekman has taught me that we can't really put a true number next to it because so much depends on what type of communication it is. In one setting it may be 55 percent, and in another it may be 80 percent. One thing we do know is, a large portion of what we "say" is through nonverbal communication.

If you are a security professional in charge of protecting your company, educating your staff, or battling the cyber war, this book can help you. You can learn how to read and use this very important aspect of communication to enhance your message, understand what people are truly saying, and even enhance your ability to test your company's defenses.

I hope you enjoy this book and that you will feel free to reach out to me and discuss these topics. Now let's move on to Chapter 1 and discuss nonverbal communication.

Building the Foundation

1

What Is Nonverbal Communication?

Emotion always has its roots in the unconscious and manifests itself in the body.

—Irene Claremont de Castillejo

My first book, *Social Engineering: The Art of Human Hacking,* touched on the subject of communication modeling. I talked about how important it is to develop and understand the model around which you and others communicate.

Communication modeling is understanding the methods used to give and receive information. For instance, if you are communicating through email the *sender* (you) has to transmit emotion, intention, and message using only words, emoticons, and phrasing. The *receiver* (recipient) has to decipher this based on their state of mind and the way they interpret your email. In the communications cycle, feedback, in its varied forms, is critical.

If you are communicating in person, on the other hand, the sender has not only the words spoken but the body language, facial expressions, and more to relay the message. This means that a social engineer needs to model their communication style, method, and content based on the manner of communication as well as the receiver.

This chapter focuses on nonverbal communication. Nonverbal communication is a rich and complex topic, so this chapter first identifies what nonverbal communication is before breaking it down into smaller subsets.

To understand nonverbal communication, you must also understand what each one of our senses adds to the way we communicate. That is the crux of this chapter. I will touch on these topics and give an overview of what comprises the whole of nonverbal communications.

For instance, suppose you are giving a speech in front of a large group. As you look into the crowd, you see some people yawning, some using their mobile devices, and some leaning on their hands with their eyelids drooping. What do these actions mean? Without any words, you probably can conclude that you are losing your audience and that they are bored and uninterested.

Why? One simple reason: nonverbal communication. Many studies attach a percentage to how much of what we communicate is nonverbal. Some say that more than 50 percent of communication is nonverbal. In my work with Dr. Ekman, I have learned that it is hard to attach a real percentage to this phenomenon because it changes according to the type of communication, its purpose, toward whom it is directed, and many other factors. However, everyone agrees that the percentage would be high if a percentage could be attached to it.

Think back to the last time you received a text message or email that you interpreted as being harsh or sarcastic, but later you found out that was not the sender's (transmitter's) intent. Why does this happen? When you are reading a message without the transmitter present, you interject your feelings and present emotional state into the message.

I remember one hectic day when my brain was going in 50 directions and I was stressed out. Someone sent me a message that said something like "I tried calling you a few times. If you decide to actually work today, give me a call." I was seeing red. How dare he accuse me of being lazy! Doesn't he know how much I've done today? I've probably accomplished more today than he has in the last three weeks! I'll give him a piece of my mind!

I wrote a long email, chewing him out. But as I reread it, I began to hear in my head how angry I sounded. I thought about who had sent the email and how we always joked around. I was stressed and under pressure and had put my emotional state on the sender of the email. Emails lack voice tone, facial expressions, and body language to help us get the message the sender is trying to send.

If I had been sitting in front of that person, I would have seen his smile and jovial nature. These would have quickly quelled any mis-impression that he had negative thoughts about my work ethic or time-management skills.

Nonverbals are such an important part of how we communicate that some people have devoted their life's work to understanding them. This book delves into the research from these people, such as Dr. Ekman, analyzing the research to understand how it applies to social engineers.

Dr. Joseph J. Campos, head of the University of California Berkeley's Institute of Human Development, along with Drs. Anderson, Witherington, Uchiyama, and Barbu-Roth, performed a "visual cliff" experiment to demonstrate the importance of nonverbal communication.[1] An infant who was

---

[1] Lejeune, L., Anderson, D. I., Campos, J. J., Witherington, D. C., Uchiyama, I., Barbu-Roth, M. (2005). "Avoidance of Heights on the Visual Cliff in Newly Walking Infants." *Infancy* 7(3), 285–298.

old enough to crawl but not old enough to speak was placed at the end of a table with a Plexiglas top and a checkerboard pattern underneath. It looked to the baby as though, halfway across, the tabletop dropped off steeply, like a tall step down, but this was an optical illusion.

At the far end, past the "dangerous cliff," was a toy. Over the edge of the table, near the toy, the baby could see the face of his or her mother. The mother was instructed to use no words, only facial expressions, to encourage her baby to come to her. When the baby arrived at the "cliff," the mother was to show a macroexpression—a very long facial expression—of either happiness or fear. If the mother was happy, she displayed a smile that produced wrinkles on the outer sides of each eye (what Dr. Ekman describes as a "sincere smile") and told the baby everything was okay, as shown in Figure 1-1. If the mother showed fear, she would pull back her lips horizontally/laterally and open her eyes wide, as shown in Figure 1-2.

When the mother showed signs of happiness, the baby was more likely not to notice the visual cliff and to crawl straight across to his or her mother. If the mother showed signs of fear, the baby displayed caution. One baby even shook his head when thinking about crossing the cliff.

Figure 1-1: How would the baby feel at seeing this expression on his mother?

Figure 1-2: How would the baby feel at seeing this expression on his mother?

This and similar experiments prove how important it is to understand the depth, seriousness, and impact that nonverbal communication has on the people we communicate with. Taking this a step further, we see how important it is to understand how professional social engineers can use nonverbals. Using this experiment as an example, if a social engineer's face shows fear when approaching a target, it will create feelings of fear in the target and cause them to wonder what is going on. If, on the other hand, the social engineer shows happiness, it is easier to develop rapport and achieve the desired goal.

So far I have classified all nonverbal communication into one large group, but this type of communication has many aspects.

The Different Aspects of Nonverbal Communication

Nonverbal communication can be broken into different aspects. Numerous researchers have spent thousands of hours dividing it into many categories. This section discusses some of the aspects I feel can really help you understand nonverbal communication.

In particular, this section discusses seven aspects of nonverbal communication: kinesics, proxemics, touch, eye contact, olfactics, adornment, and facial expressions. The following sections briefly describe each.

Kinesics

Kinesics is defined as "a systematic study of the relationship between nonlinguistic body motions (as blushes, shrugs, or eye movement) and communication."

In essence, this term describes body language and how our bodies can give away the emotion we are feeling. Dr. Ekman wrote a paper in 1975 called "Communicative Body Movements" that focused on the work of Dr. David Efron from the 1940s. It discussed four areas of kinesics: emblems, illustrators, manipulators, and one I call RSVP. I will briefly describe these here and then explain in much more detail in Chapter 3.

Emblems

An emblem is a nonverbal movement that often involves the hands. Emblems have some very distinct aspects.

Imagine this scenario: From across the room, your friend notices you look a little pale, and she mouths, "Are you okay?" What gesture or gestures does she use—a thumbs-up with a shrug? How do you respond? Maybe you rub your stomach and give a thumbs-down motion. What are you saying? Your stomach is upset. You just had a small conversation with few or no words, using emblems.

Also, ponder the second aspect. If your conversation had taken place in the Middle East, you might not have used a thumbs-up emblem, because it has a completely different meaning in that part of the world. The emblems shown in Figures 1-3 and 1-4 change meaning depending on where they are used.

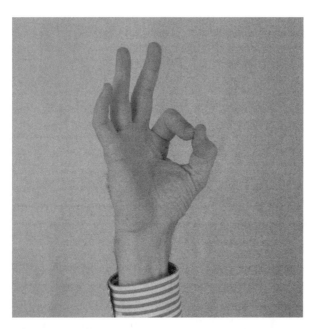

Figure 1-3: "Everything is okay," or a derogatory statement?

Figure 1-4: Depending on where in the world you make this gesture, it could be benign or offensive.

Very much like the words you use, which you are aware of, we are aware of the emblems we use when we are speaking, because they are deliberate. And just as "slips of the tongue" can occur, emblem slips can happen in conversation.

Think about some of the emblems you have seen and what they mean.

In the US, the emblem shown in Figure 1-3 communicates that everything is good, but in the Middle East, parts of Africa, and other lands, it's an offensive gesture.

I will dive deeper into this topic in Chapter 3 because as a social engineer, you should understand emblems and their meanings depending on the country, culture, or people you are trying to influence. Using the wrong emblem at the wrong time can quickly change your communication from something influential to something insulting.

Illustrators

In 1972, Dr. Ekman wrote a paper called "Hand Movements."[2] It defined illustrators as "those acts which are intimately related on a moment-to-moment basis with speech, with phrasing, content, voice contours, loudness, etc." (p. 358)

In other words, illustrators are gestures that usually augment what is being said. They are somewhat similar to emblems, although illustrators usually are used peripherally and without awareness.

When someone says "Aha!" or yells "Wait!," what illustrator do you imagine being used? Or when someone says, "I headed north of the mountain and then drove on a really winding road for about three hours," what illustrators do you imagine being used? You probably can picture how those conversations would go. You have seen and used illustrators many times.

Manipulators

A manipulator is any movement that involves a manipulation or grooming of a body part or article of clothing due to nervousness or discomfort

---

[2] Ekman, P. (1972, December). "Hand Movements." *Journal of Communication* 22(4), pp. 353–374.

or as a link to relaxation and comfort. Examples include playing with your ring or cuffs, rubbing your hands together, adjusting your buttons or shirt, and fixing your hair.

Dr. Ekman's work made one thing very clear, and I reiterate this point often: These and other cues are not automatic signs of deception. They may indicate that the person is uncomfortable with the situation, the other person, the questions, or the environment, and they may be linked to deception. But this doesn't mean that if someone starts using manipulators he or she is a liar.

In a social engineering context, manipulators help you see if someone is comfortable or showing signs of discomfort. In addition, knowing how the human mind perceives these signals allows a social engineer to use them to cause a feeling in his or her targets.

RSVP

Our verbal style and content comprise another emblem that is important to focus on. RSVP stands for rhythm, speed, volume, and pitch. This refers not to the actual words that are used but to everything else surrounding those words.

The rhythm a person uses when speaking can tell us if he is nervous, calm, confident, or feeling other emotions.

The speed at which he speaks can indicate his feelings, where he is from, and how much confidence he has in what he is saying.

Volume can give clues about the content of what is being said. Is he whispering or speaking too loudly? These things can indicate what type of person we are dealing with. A rise in volume may indicate anger.

Pitch is likewise important, because it can indicate comfort and/or discomfort. A rise in pitch may indicate fear; a drop in pitch may indicate sadness or uncertainty.

Noticing things such as pauses, repetition, and changes in words or tones can help us understand what the person is really trying to say.

Here are some things to watch for:

- **Change of pronouns (verbal style):** If the person starts out saying "I" but then changes to "we" and "us," this may indicate a level of deception. Even if changing pronouns is not deceptive, it is a good indicator for us to listen more closely for why the story has changed.

■ **Increase in stuttering or word repetition (verbal style):** This may indicate increased anxiety or stress. One word of caution: Without a baseline, you can't know if the person stutters as a part of his or her normal speech patterns, so use this indicator with caution.

■ **Change in voice tone:** Tone can indicate much emotion. Happiness, disgust, anger, and contempt all can come across in your tone. As a test, the next time you see your dog, look at him sternly, angrily shout, "I love you!," and watch as he runs to a corner. The words are not important, but the tone and expressions are.

■ **Verbal hedges:** When someone doesn't want to answer a question, he or she will "hedge," trying to avoid the question.

■ **The Pause:** A pause indicates cognitive load and may also include eye movement. In simplest terms, the paused speaker is formulating a response. For the interviewer, the issue is whether the pause is recall memory or to fabricate a story. Here's an important axiom: *Do not interrupt the pause.* Too often, the interviewer fills the pause, perhaps taking the speaker off the hook, or inserts leading questions or comments that may influence the speaker.

Learning to observe these signs in others and being aware of how they spill over into your own speech can help you as a communicator and a social engineer. You can figure out how to determine levels of comfort and discomfort as well as nonverbal cues to a person's true emotional state.

The next aspect of nonverbal communication takes a trip back in time to some research conducted in the 1950s.

Proxemics

In the 1950s researcher Dr. Edward Hall coined the term *proxemics*, which concerns our use of the space around us and various differences that can indicate comfort or discomfort.

The phrase "personal space" applies to proxemics. In his research, Dr. Hall talked about four areas:

- **Public space:** Focusing on Western cultures, he found that a range of 12 to 25 feet is the acceptable separation from, for example, an audience and a speaker. Think about the last time you attended a concert or saw the president speak on TV. You probably noticed a level of public space that was considered acceptable.
- **Social space:** This is the space that is considered acceptable in social settings. Try to remember the last time you were at the beach, sitting on a beach towel with your family. How close would be acceptable for someone to come set up next to you? Dr. Hall says somewhere between 4 and 10 feet.
- **Personal space:** This is what we consider reasonable when interacting with family or friends. It is also acceptable space when waiting in line. This ranges from 2 to 4 feet.
- **Intimate space:** This space is reserved for those we let touch us, whisper to us, and be intimate with us. This is less than 1 foot.

Imagine you are in line at the ATM, and the person behind you comes within a few inches of you. When you move, he moves. You can feel his breath on the back of your neck. Creeped out? This stranger has violated your intimate space.

Yet in the Middle East, what they consider to be social space is what American citizens consider to be intimate space. If you conducted business there, as an American, you might find yourself constantly backing up if you were unaware of the customs. Some European cultures, on the other hand, have personal space requirements that are closer to our social space. It is important to understand and remember these differences when interacting with other cultures. Again, they can help you notice signs of discomfort or comfort.

Touch

Touch is an integral part of the human experience. We learn so much from it. Imagine how much trouble we would be in if we couldn't feel heat, cold, sharpness, and so on. Our sense of touch goes a long way in communicating to our brains what's going on around us.

In the same way, touch can communicate emotions to others and create a sense of trust in them. Research conducted at the Université de Bretagne-Sud in Vannes, France showed that simply touching a complete stranger on the arm increased the likelihood of one stranger helping another from 63 percent to 90 percent.[3]

Of course, other factors come into play, such as cultural differences, age, gender, and background. Despite all that, the study helps social engineers understand how the power of nonsexual touch can create an atmosphere of compliance. When used properly, this aspect of nonverbal communication can open doors for the social engineer.

Dr. Paul Zak, a professor of macroeconomics and neuroscience at Claremont University, researched oxytocin, a naturally occurring chemical in the brain that helps people feel trust. He found that one of the key ways to release oxytocin is through a simple hug. A simple touch between two people, if done right, can release a chemical that creates an environment amenable to trust and rapport building—two key elements for any social engineer. He writes about this in his book called *The Moral Molecule*, and also discussed this topic on my podcast.

Eye Contact

You may have heard that "The eyes are the windows to the soul." This statement is true when we discuss how this area of nonverbal communication affects how we view the emotional state of other people.

Consider Figure 1-5. Which set of eyes shows someone who is happy, and which shows someone who is afraid? Both pictures are of the same woman, yet the difference is clear.

In this case, you don't need words—you don't even need the rest of the face; all you need are the eyes. This illustrates how important the eyes are to communication.

[3] "Tactile Contact and Spontaneous Help: An Evaluation in a Natural Setting" by Nicholas Geuguen and Jacques Fischer-Lokou. *The Journal of Social Psychology*, 2003, 143(6), 785–787.

Figure 1-5: Which expression is happy, and which is full of fear?

Some people believe you can tell if someone is lying based on the direction in which he looks, but recent studies have disproven that theory. Nevertheless, you can spot many things in regards to the eyes and levels of comfort or discomfort.

The topic of eye contact interests me. I tend to learn more easily when someone tells me a fact. Therefore, I tend to look away when someone is talking. Though I may appear not to be paying attention, I am actively listening. However, the person I am speaking to may not feel that way. Even though I am not being deceptive or rude, it is culturally accepted that when you're being spoken to, a certain amount of eye contact is proper.

Being conscious of eye contact can benefit the social engineer. At the same time, to not fall into the trap of thinking that everyone who looks away is lying. Do notice someone who shifts his or her eyes a lot or who cannot look at you when speaking. Noticing areas of discomfort can go a long way toward reading the person's emotional state.

In one of my conversations with Dr. Ekman, when I asked about the importance of eye contact, he said, "It can have many different meanings, depending on the context. It can assert dominance, initiate a flirtation, or be a sign that someone is lying, who mistakenly believes that only liars look away when they talk."

Olfactics

Olfactics is the study of smell in relation to nonverbal communication. Our bodies associate certain smells with emotions and feelings. Some smells can be powerful triggers for memories of and emotions toward people, events, or things.

Think of a food you love to smell when it's cooking. When you smell it, what happens? Conversely, what happens when you smell something that once made you sick, even to the point of vomiting? Even thinking about it now may cause your face to wrinkle in disgust.

Smell is a powerful force. Pheromones can attract the opposite sex and even induce other emotions, such as fear.

How does this apply to the social engineer? It is important to be aware of how we smell. Strong perfumes or colognes can be offensive to some people. Body odor also can be offensive, so social engineers should never subject their targets to body odors (unless your pretext is one that might allow for that).

Adornment

See if you can answer these questions:

> A woman in brown slacks, a brown shirt, and a brown ball cap drives up to your business and delivers some boxes. Who does she work for?
>
> A young male pulls up to your house in jeans and a red-and-blue shirt, carrying a square box. Who does he work for?
>
> A man is wearing a shirt with his name on it, his hands are covered in oil and grease, and he is wearing a ball cap. What does he do?

You probably can figure out that these describe a UPS delivery person, a pizza delivery guy, and a mechanic. Why? Adornment, or their clothing. Clothing, jewelry, make up, and even hair can set us apart and tells people all about us without words.

In one engagement I had to "break into" a few warehouses. I needed to do this not by scaling fences or picking locks, but by getting the employees to let me in willingly. I had a shirt made up with my "name" on it and a matching hat, and I went to the warehouse. I said I was from their waste management company and I needed to check their trash compactor. No one asked me for ID, and no one called the local office. Why? My outfit told the story. And because the story matched what I said, no one stopped me.

One time I interviewed radio host Tom Mischke about how he got his job. He started his career as a prank caller to a local radio station, pretending to be certain characters. Eventually these characters became pretty well known in his area, so he began to have set times to call in and perform these characters for the listeners. He told me he spent time as each character, even going as far as dressing how he thought the character would dress. This story helps us understand how powerful adornment or clothing is to the social engineer. This point was highlighted by a group of researchers who set up some experiments involving "enclothed cognition."[4]

They showed volunteers two white coats—one commonly worn by a doctor, and another by a painter. The first test was to find out how this group viewed the two different coats. Most participants felt that the doctor's coat showed focus, attentiveness, caution, and responsibility, whereas the painter's coat did not suggest these traits.

They ran a few experiments. First they tested to see if having the participants wear a lab coat made a difference. Then they also changed what it stood for. The interesting part of the study is that both coats were the same, but the researchers just told the subjects they had different roles.

It appears their hypothesis was correct. Again quoting this study and the term they coined, enclothed cognition:

The current research provides initial support for our enclothed cognition perspective that clothes can have profound and systematic psychological and behavioral consequences for their wearers. In Experiment 1, participants who wore a lab coat displayed increased selective attention compared to participants who wore their regular clothes. In Experiments 2 and 3, we found robust evidence that this influence of clothing depends

---

[4] Adam, H. & Galinsky, A. D. (2012). "Enclothed cognition." *Journal of Experimental Social Psychology*. doi: 10.1016/j.jesp.2012.02.008.

on both whether the clothes are worn and the symbolic meaning of the clothes. When the coat was associated with a doctor but not worn, there was no increase in sustained attention. When the coat was worn but not associated with a doctor, there was no increase in sustained attention. Only when a) participants were wearing the coat and b) it was associated with a doctor did sustained attention increase. These results suggest a basic principle of enclothed cognition: It involves the co-occurrence of two independent factors—the symbolic meaning of the clothes and the physical experience of wearing them (Adam & Galinsky).

These conclusions point to the power of clothes and adornment for the social engineer in two ways. First, the clothes the social engineer chooses to wear, and second, determining a target's thoughts about themselves based on their clothing.

Facial Expressions

Chapter 5 discusses this topic in much more depth. The human face holds a lot of information about what we are feeling; it can tell a whole story without words. As I discussed in *Social Engineering*, learning to read facial expressions can enhance your ability to communicate clearly. Based on Dr. Ekman's research, Chapter 5 of this book is all about decoding the face, what each expression looks like, and what it can mean to you.

Many people believe you should focus only on the face or only on the body or only on the hands. But if there is one thing I learned in my couple of years with Dr. Ekman, it is that reading people is a whole package. The face may display an emotion, but that might be inconsistent with what you see in the body and hands and hear in the words. Learning to read the person as a whole is a talent that can make or break the social engineer.

The following exercise, taken from Dr. Ekman's work and *Social Engineering*, will help solidify this point. For each picture shown in Figure 1-6, decide what emotion you think is displayed.

Figure 1-6: What emotion do you think each picture represents?

Being able to read these emotions and therefore understand what someone may be feeling (notice I said *what*, not *why*) can help you adjust your approach or opening statement to be more attractive to that person.

You probably don't want to antagonize the person at the bottom right. You might want to exercise some extra humility when dealing with the person second from left in the top row. If you see the expression at the top, third from the left, you might want to find out what is disgusting him. You get the point: Examining facial expressions can help you adjust and change your approaches.

Years of research have revealed that these expressions are universal. Across gender, culture, race, and demographics are base emotions that we all feel and express the same way. Of course, the reasons for those emotions change depending on those very same things.

How to Use This Information

The rest of this book digs a little deeper into these areas. You will see how you, as a social engineer, communicator, and human being, can use each of these cues to better understand the people around you.

Personally, I have found it exhilarating and enlightening to learn these things. To be able to look across the room and see that someone may be feeling sad or angry gives me insight into my family, friends, and others. Stepping away from the role of social engineer for a moment, I find this information enlightening because it helps me be more understanding. Instead of thinking, "Why would she say something like that to me?" or "Why would he act that way? What did I do to deserve that?," I took the "me" and "I" out of the equation and began to understand what the person may be feeling. Doing so helped me understand that it isn't all about me, as my good friend Robin Dreeke would say. It's about understanding them.

Let me give you a short example of why this is so powerful. I was standing in Heathrow airport waiting for my turn at the customs officer. There are 27 banks of stations and yet only three people working. Tensions in the line are mounting and then two officers go on break, leaving one customs officer. One of the TV monitors flashes a message stating that if you have a complaint to give it to one of the people working there as complaints can help them improve.

I overheard a few people complaining to a man who appeared to be a manager. I must admit, I was pretty heated myself. I had another flight and was running late. I had eyed up the manager and determined when I got closer I would "file my complaint." He came strolling across the floor as now a few returned from break. What I saw changed my plans. His fists where tightly clenched, showing white knuckles. His jaw was tight and his lips pressed together. His arms were stiff and his walk was heavy. What do you think?

He wasn't just angry—he was infuriated. I didn't know why just yet, but I determined if I were to complain, he was not the right guy and this was not the right time. Being able to see this body language and facial expressions saved me from making a grave mistake in judgment.

As I got closer to the front in line I heard him say to his co-worker, "Just because he works for the American government he thinks he can come to *my* country and speak to *me* that way?!? He needs to remember while he's here he's only a visitor, and that is a privilege that can be removed!"

Sure enough, I now had the proof needed that his anger was blazing and my minor complaint would not have "improved the quality of their service" but probably only landed me in some trouble, delays, and more problems.

As this simple story defines, once we open our minds to understanding the other person, what makes her tick, why she reacts a certain way, and why she says or does certain things, we begin to really understand her. This makes me recall another situation I was in recently where I did something very thoughtless. I said something that hurt a close friend. When she came to talk to me about it, I felt I was being attacked, and I became defensive. I made the situation all about me and reacted with a very self-protective attitude. Notice just the few sentences above are littered with "me's" and "I's." That is where I was focused, not on her feelings but mine.

Shortly afterward, I saw this person again. Seeing her face made me happy, although nervous. She looked very sad. Not angry, just sad. As I approached her, her hips and feet were facing away from me. We exchanged pleasantries. I didn't understand everything at the time it happened, but shortly thereafter I reflected on the situation. The sadness on her face and her body language indicated she was uncomfortable and didn't want to be in that situation.

Why am I telling you about this mistake I made? Understanding how to read people helped me in this situation to see that I did not anger my friend, but instead hurt her. She may have felt angry at first, but the emotion I had left her with was sadness. It took away my need to be self-protective and to see what I had done and how it affected her.

Being able to see, read, and react to true emotion is powerful. But any power needs to be wielded properly. Maybe the best way to express what I want to say here can be taken from Dr. Ekman's book *Emotions Revealed*[5]. He states the following about reading others' emotions: "Often the best course is to say nothing about what you have seen. Instead, be alert to the possibilities. … How you respond depends on the nature of your relationship, its past history and intended future, and your

---

[5] Ekman, Paul. (2003). Emotions Revealed: Recognizing Faces and Feelings to Improve Communication and Emotional Life. New York: Times Books.

knowledge of that person. You may not always be entitled to comment, even vaguely, on the emotion you have detected" (230).

Interesting words, aren't they?

Summary

Considering that a large portion of what we communicate is not spoken but rather conveyed through our face, body, hands, feet, and legs, we should spend considerable time trying to understand nonverbal communication. But why should we do so in a book on social engineering?

Scammers, con artists, and social engineers have long been using these skills. They can build rapport, see when their mark is drawn in, and see when they have him on the hook. In essence, they can read the nonverbal cues that their target gives off.

As a social engineering professional, I find that it is important to understand these things—not just so that I can use them to complete my pretext, but so that I can use them to read my target's emotional state and see how I'm doing.

Before we go into the details, we need to discuss what social engineering is and why you should be aware of its malicious uses.

2

What Is Social Engineering?

Enlightenment is not imagining figures of light but making the darkness conscious.

—*Carl Gustav*

define social engineering as any act that influences someone to take an action that may or may not be in his or her best interest. As mentioned briefly in Chapter 1, I once was hired to infiltrate warehouses without breaking and entering. To do so, I used the social engineering methods of pretexting, role playing, and three or four different aspects of influence. My intent was to test the company's defenses to see if the employees followed policy. I also tried to take pictures of the exits, camera locations, and other aspects that a real criminal would use to come back later and break in. A typical scenario went something like this:

I drove to the warehouse and pressed the intercom button at the front door. I said, "Hi, this is Paul from your waste company. I need to check the serial number on your trash compactor."

The door buzzed, and I was let into the inner area of the warehouse. I faced a wall-to-wall, floor-to-ceiling metal mantrap. A security guard looked in and said, "Hold on a minute. The floor manager is coming to escort you."

A few minutes later, Roy, the floor manager, came out to greet me. I was buzzed through the ominous-looking mantrap and was sent to the security guard desk. The security guard asked for my ID. I looked at him and then at the mantrap and said, "I left my wallet in my car. But I do have my company ID. Is that okay?" The security guard photocopied my company ID and gave me a badge. Roy then took me to the compactor.

After a few seconds, I said, "You're in luck. This number is not on the list."

"What does that mean?" Roy asked.

"You don't have a bad motor, so this compactor should be in top shape."

On the walk back, I suddenly exclaimed, "Dang it! I left my phone on top of the compactor. I need to run back and get it."

A few minutes later, I met Roy in the office, shook his hand, returned the visitor ID, and left the building.

In addition to showing that corporate policy might need better enforcement, I left the building with a phone full of pictures of security camera locations, exits, and where the "goods" are stored.

Social engineering doesn't always involve trickery or deceit. Instead, it is more about how we conduct our social interactions on a daily basis. It is about how we communicate, talk, and get our point across to people with whom we interact.

In my first book, *Social Engineering: The Art of Human* Hacking (Wiley, 2011). I broke down all the physical, psychological, and personal tools someone needs to become a master social engineer. Rather than recap the whole book here, this chapter gives a brief overview of techniques and methods used by a social engineer.

Keep in mind that it is vital for the social engineer to become part of the same "tribe" as the target. A tribe can involve a workplace, beliefs, clothing, music—anything that causes people to join a group. If you can utilize the skills outlined in the following sections, you can become part of the target's tribe. Once that occurs, gathering information or gaining access is much simpler.

Information Gathering

Information is the lifeblood of the social engineer. The more information the social engineer has, the more vectors (or, methods of infiltration), he can develop, the more he understands the target, and the more he can understand the target's weaknesses and strengths.

Information gathering can be web-based, using tools such as Google dorking and Maltego. It also can involve in-person gathering, such as taking pictures, location scoping, and elicitation.

The power of the internet makes gathering information much easier nowadays, and it means that a social engineer can obtain a very large quantity of data. Learning how to categorize and store this information is very important. I have a practice of developing DAPs (detailed action plans) on my targets that involve information found, attitudes or actions observed, and how this info was gathered. I then correlate that with vectors I want to use and that becomes a plan of action for each target.

Social engineer and ethical-hacker-turned-philanthropist Johnny Long developed the initial Google Hacking Database, which is a list of searches that one can run in Google to find all sorts of juicy information. In the last few years, the folks at Offensive Security have taken over this project and it now lives at www.exploit-db.com.

In addition to tools like this there are others like Maltego, which allows you to gather data on people, websites, or companies and categorizes it in a graphical format that is easy to read and use. More information can be found at www.paterva.com.

Recently a couple of other tools I have found very useful are Google Maps or Bing Maps. When you zoom in close enough, each of these websites will show you a "street view" of the location. If you approach a building or location and already know the layout, the fencing, the camera locations, and more, it saves you the time of having to figure this all out on the spot.

However a social engineer gathers information, the rule of thumb should be "no information is useless." Even the littlest pieces of information can go a long way into the success of an engagement.

Pretexting

Your pretext is the person you will portray—the act you will put on. It is somewhat like Method acting—you become the person you are pretending to be. Clothing, ID, body language, and knowledge all play a role in making a pretext believable.

In the example at the beginning of this chapter, my pretext was "Paul the waste company employee." To successfully carry out my pretext, I needed to do some planning. I had to make sure my clothing convinced my targets I was who I said I was. Just as I mentioned in Chapter 1 when I spoke about "enclothed cognition" I had to make sure my clothing made me feel the part and portrayed the right message too.

My ID had to be realistic. My body language had to suggest that I was a blue-collar worker and not upper management. I also needed knowledge of the artifacts I was using to prove my pretext. I had to know about trash compactors, where the serial numbers were located, what I would be looking for, and any tools needed to do my "job."

In the same way, a pretext is not always in person. In a five-day class I teach, I send the students out each night to gather small pieces of information from people in the public to show them how using these skills can develop rapport, generate trust, and result in information sharing very fast. During one particular class I had a group of students get together in their hotel room and gather information by pretending to be a call center.

To complete the pretext they downloaded an app called "Thriving Office" that played office sounds in the background. One of their cell phones played these sounds while the others made calls. For the person on the other end of the phone the pretext was complete as they heard a "call center."

Whether in person, over the phone, or through email, a social engineer's pretext needs to encompass clothing, language and words choice, sounds, and every aspect of the method of communication to prove to the target that the social engineer is who he says he is.

Elicitation

Elicitation is the art of getting information without asking direct questions—just carrying on normal conversation. Elicitation is talking to your target about his or her life, family, and job. You build rapport with your target (see the next section) and get him or her to like you, open up, and offer details you can use. Such a simple explanation, but one of the most important aspects of social engineering.

At the end of this book, I will spend some considerable time discussing how nonverbal communication affects elicitation and can enhance your ability to be a master elicitor.

Rapport

My good friend and author Robin Dreeke defines and discusses rapport-building skills in his book *It's Not All About "Me."* He can quickly teach anyone the best techniques for making people feel liked, which creates an atmosphere of trust. That trust then causes them to talk and give away information that may be valuable. That trust also can cause someone to take action, such as clicking a bad link or letting a social engineer through a door.

Rapport is the feeling of closeness or trust that is developed when psychologically someone opens up and is now willing to trust you with information about their lives.

Robin breaks building rapport down into 10 different methods. Quickly they are:

- **Artificial time constraints**: Letting people know you will only "bother" them for a very brief period of time
- **Accommodating nonverbals**: Making sure your nonverbals match your words or there will be red flags raised
- **Slower rate of speech**: Speaking slow enough not to appear nervous
- **Sympathy themes**: Using the powerful words, "Can you help me?"
- **Ego suspension**: This powerful aspect is merely suspending your own ego to let others be right, even if they aren't.
- **Validation**: Using warm and genuine accommodation of a person's knowledge, skills or person
- **Asking how, when, or why questions**: Open ended questions that elicit longer responses
- **Quid pro quo**: Giving a little info out to make the person feel comfortable sharing their info
- **Reciprocal altruism**: Giving a gift to get a gift
- **Manage expectations**: To not become greedy and to realize when something isn't working and make a change

Each of these 10 aspects is powerful and can be part of an effective social engineer's arsenal.

Influence/Manipulation

I define "influence" as "getting someone to *want* to do what you want them to do." In essence, your target goes along willingly, as if it was their idea and something they wanted to be a part of all along.

One of the greatest minds in regards to this topic is Dr. Robert Cialdini. He spent his life studying influence and how it works.

Dr. Robert Cialdini defines eight aspects of influence:

- **Reciprocity** is creating a feeling of indebtedness by being the first to give something away.

- **Obligation** influences someone to take action based on a feeling, whether this is the social norm of showing gratitude or the feeling that we owe someone something.

- **Concession** is getting someone to give you smaller answers. Giving in and answering basic questions leads the target down the path to answering bigger ones.

- **Scarcity**: When people are convinced that the item or information in question is hard to come by, running out, or may be gone forever, it becomes scarce and therefore more valuable.

- **Authority** plays on our innate desire to obey and follow direction, especially from those in a higher position.

- **Consistency and commitment** are involved when a target starts down a path. She wants to remain consistent in her responses. This creates a feeling of commitment to continue giving consistent answers.

- **Liking** means that people like those who like them. If our targets feel liked, they will like us in return and give us the information we need.

- **Social proof** means that if everyone else is doing it, it must be okay. This principle plays on the feeling that being part of the group is important.

Learning to master, understand, and use these eight principles can make you a master social engineer. Manipulation is not much different than influence. As a matter of fact, when you analyze the principles of manipulation, they are very similar to influence. Telling the two apart is critically important, though. Whereas influence is getting a person to want to do what you want them to do, manipulation is getting a person to do something they don't want to do.

In essence, the goal when you influence someone is to always try to make him or her feel better for having met you. When you manipulate someone, there is no goal that is focused on their feelings; the goal is to get what you want, regardless of how the subject feels.

As a social engineer, I try never to employ manipulation as it leaves my clients feeling bad, ruins our relationship and does not open up the employees to training. Instead I always try to employ influence because it opens the client up to advice, training, and change.

A great illustration that a good friend told me once is that manipulation is like getting your child to accept the shot they need. The medicine will make them feel better but the shot may sting a bit. As a professional social engineer, regardless of how I get you to give up information, I am sure it will sting a bit, but the goal is to try to use the method of least sting so you accept it and can improve your security posture.

Framing

Just as a house's frame is its basic structure, a person's *frame* is her emotional, psychological, and personal and family history. What causes her to think, act, and talk the way she does? These motivations are a person's frame.

What someone has experienced throughout her life alters how she perceives the world around her and how she reacts to events. If a social engineer can begin to understand a person's frame, he can begin building a bridge between his frame and the target's frame.

The easiest way to do this is to find common ground and then build rapport. Doing so makes bridging the two frames much easier. As soon as the frames are bridged, the target and the social engineer become part of the same "tribe," and it is easier to gather intel from that target.

Nonverbal Communications

Chapter 1 described nonverbal communication (also called nonverbals) in detail. As I discussed in my first book, this topic really changed how we view social engineering. Combining nonverbals with the other aspects just described can make anyone an amazing social engineer.

Nonverbals make up a large portion of how we communicate. What we say is either confirmed or contradicted by how we say it and how we look when we say it. Gaining the ability to detect, analyze, and read microexpressions, macroexpressions, subtle microexpressions, conversational signals, and body language can help you as a social engineer understand the emotional makeup of your target.

Understanding your target's emotional state before you engage with him or her can help you alter your approach, your opening, and the types of questions you ask and conversations you have.

My first book barely scratched the surface of this topic. I covered only the basics of facial expressions. This book, with the help of Dr. Paul Ekman, delves deeply into the face, hands, body, legs, and torso. I explain how each of these areas gives us insights into our targets' emotions.

First we need to discuss how nonverbal communications play into the different types of social engineering.

The Three Basic Forms of Social Engineering

Social engineering in its malicious form is usually categorized into three different areas. It is important for you to understand the differences among the three, because nonverbals play a role in each. Let's take a look at each: phishing, phone elicitation, and impersonation.

Become Phishers of Men

The most widely used form of social engineering is phishing—the sending of either mass or targeted emails that contain malicious files, links, or instructions. If clicked, opened, or followed, those aspects of a phish cause breaches, data loss, and many other problems.

One example of phishing was in the news when I wrote this chapter. An executive at Coca-Cola received an email instructing him to open a file from the CEO regarding energy conservation, an initiative that this company was pushing. That email and its attachment were not legitimate. By opening the file, the executive allowed a program to be run on his computer, giving the hackers remote access to his machine. This led to a full network compromise that was not discovered for many months.

Phishing emails are so prevalent that one group claims that one out of every 300 emails is a phish. This doesn't even begin to cover when the phish are targeted attacks. When a social engineer targets a particular person, he uses spear phishing—very personalized emails that contain details about the person's likes or dislikes. Or he may use what is called whaling, in which a spear phish is sent to a high-profile target, such as the CEO of a large bank.

Whatever method is used, the social engineer writes emails that use fear, curiosity, or authority to get the reader to perform an action that is not in his or her best interest.

Let's look at a phish and analyze why phishing is such an effective tactic. Currently one of the most widely used phish is geared toward Facebook. With over a billion users, Facebook is an attractive target. Take a look at Figure 2-1.

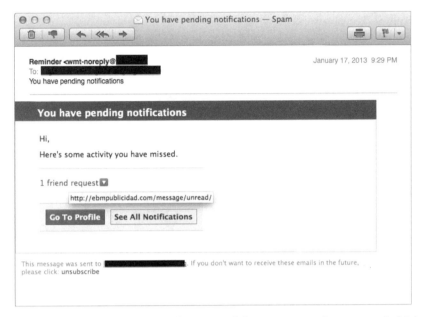

Figure 2-1: Faking Facebook is one of the most popular types of phishes.

There are a few key things to notice with this type of phish. First, it works because it looks like a real Facebook email. It has the same layout and colors. It is simple and not overdone. In addition, the subject line is ripped from actual Facebook emails.

A few clues give away this email as false:

- The "from" address is not Facebook. Sometimes a social engineer will use facbook.com or faceboook.com or facebook.co—little changes that may go widely unnoticed.
- The greeting is generic; it just says "Hi." Usually it would have your name or username.
- The big clue that often goes unnoticed is the link. When you hover the mouse pointer over the link, you see that it is not going to Facebook at all. Instead, it is going to the social engineer's website.
- This particular email is quite smart because the link, the buttons, and even the unsubscribe link all lead to a malicious site.

Another example of the seriousness of malicious phishing is a fake PayPal email, as shown in Figure 2-2.

Figure 2-2: PayPal is widely used in phishing attacks.

These emails affect us because they hit us in the wallet—or so we are led to believe. The fear that someone may have accessed and stolen our funds is enough to make us click a link and quickly log into our account to verify. And this is just what the attacker wants us to do. Often a fake website, a fake login, and little scripts harvest the credentials you enter. When the attacker has these credentials, he logs in and then does the very thing that created fear in you: steals your money.

Using Nonverbal Communication in Phishing

At first it may seem next to impossible to understand how nonverbal communication is used when it comes to the written word. Yet consider the concept of framing, which is the structure upon which a person's mental and psychological house is built. The social engineer wants to alter that frame and cause the target to think, feel, and react in the frame of the social engineer. This is called frame bridging. One person builds a "bridge" between his frame and the frame of the other person, making it easier for the second person to meet him in the middle or find that common ground.

One of the main rules of framing is that any words we use evoke the frame. Our mind thinks in pictures, so the words we use create picture scenarios in our minds. Those pictures create emotional reactions, and those reactions are what cause the target to take the action that may or may not be in his or her best interest.

A malicious social engineer wants to create a set of emotional triggers in, for example, an email that will make the target perform that action. In many cases the malicious social engineer uses the emotions of fear (of loss, theft, and so on) or sadness (as it is linked with empathy and the "help me" plea) to elicit the responses he wants.

Statements such as "This must be completed in 24 hours or your account will be suspended" elicit a fear response. Combine that with the possibility that your account may have been used without your knowledge, and you have a perfect recipe for fear-based response. It is based on words, and those words paint a picture in your mind, and that picture causes the emotional reaction.

Another aspect is the use of emoticons, which are used more and more in texts, emails, and instant messages. Audrey Nelson, PhD, author of *The Gender Communication Handbook: Conquering Conversational Collisions Between Men and Women*, talks about emoticons as used in written communications. She defines emoticons as "nonverbal written indicators of emotions."

Which of the following softens the reader?

■ Wow! You really didn't think that through!
■ Wow! You really didn't think that through! ☹
■ Wow! You really didn't think that through! ☺

The use of the smiley face in the third example means that the statement is meant not as a criticism but as a joke. The emotion aimed at the target can affect how that person reacts to the message. Emoticons are used not so much in fear-based emails but in phishing emails that pretend to be from friends (such as Facebook friend emails) or potential romantic partners (such as emails from popular dating websites). In these scenarios, emoticons are used to make the sender appear to be happy, friendly, and open.

When The Phone Is More Dangerous Than Malware

The second most commonly used form of social engineering is phone elicitation. In the last 18 to 24 months, hacktivist attacks on large companies have used an increasing amount of phone elicitation. In one such case, the hacker group UG-NAZI launched an attack against a web-based invoicing company. UG-NAZI did extensive information gathering on the database administrator of this company and then placed one phone call to their tech support company requesting a password reset. Because this group had all sorts of information on the DB admin, they were able to answer the security questions and reset the password.

The result? UG-NAZI downloaded gigabytes of customer credit card numbers and then erased their servers for fun. This is just one of a dozen such stories in the recent news.

Why has the number of phone-based attacks increased? First, caller-ID spoofing, as it is often called, is cheap and easy. Spoofing, or making it appear you are calling from a number you are not calling from, the number from which the call originated means that the social engineer can fake any number he wants. He can place a call that the recipient will think is coming from tech support, a vendor, or even the president of the United States. Caller-ID spoofing creates an atmosphere of trust quickly because the number "proves" the caller is trustworthy.

Second, it's easy. The social engineer doesn't need to be present or even be in the same country to use the phone to elicit information. With a bit of practice, he can create a believable storyline and establish a decent level of trust with the target.

In one engagement I did, we used a three-layered attack. The first stage was a phish we sent to employees of the target company, offering a free iPhone 5 (the newest phone at the time) to be entered in the drawing they had to fill out a form with their domain login credentials. Hundreds of employees filled out the form.

Stage two was to call these people and tell them they had been victims of a phish. As my pretext, I became "Paul," the tech support guy from their company. I told them we had placed a tracker on their machine and we needed them to run an executable file to remove it. The executable was not a cleaning tool but a malicious file that would give us remote access to their computers. Out of all the calls I made that day, about 98 percent of the people contacted complied with the request without questioning me. For those who did, I simply told them I was from tech support and we must continue.

In the 1960s, psychologist Stanley Milgram conducted an experiment to test people's susceptibility to listen to authority even when it went against their moral judgment. As volunteers were asked to shock other people for wrong answers, the viewer can see an increase in discomfort as the other person's pain increased. The "researcher" was instructed to say, "The experiment must continue. Please go on."

Much like that famous obedience experiment, my only statements were along the lines of "We must clean the system" and "If we don't do this, it may cause more problems on the network." I was to state this with confidence and authority.

At this point in the penetration test, the point was proven, but the team and I wanted to try one more test, now that malicious software was loaded on the computers. I called tech support, posing as the employee I had just spoken to about running the executable file. I told tech support that my VPN credentials had been deleted, so I needed them again. Having this information would allow me into the most secure parts of the network.

The phone call went like this:

"Tech support. Sylvia speaking. How can I help you?"

I had spoofed my number so that the call appeared to come from the office of the person I was pretexting as. "Hi. This is James. I just loaded something on my machine that I shouldn't have. When I ran the virus scan to clean it off, it also erased my VPN credentials. Can you please give me the credentials again?"

"Sure, I can help you. Please tell me your full name."

"James Smith. You can call me Jim."

"Jim? Smith?"

"Yes."

"Don't you recognize my voice? This is Sylvia."

I had to think fast. I didn't know what relationship these two had, and one wrong word might blow my cover. "Sylvia, I'm sorry. I'm so stressed. I clicked on this phish and then loaded some bad software. When I tried to clean it, it messed up my machine. My head is spinning. I think I'm getting a cold; that's why my voice sounds different. And, on top of everything else, I lost my VPN creds. Forgive me and can you please help me?"

"Sure. No problem, Jim. Let me pull up your credentials."

A few seconds later, I was handed the keys to the kingdom. Why did this work so well? I didn't have to prove who I was because I was on a phone with the right number, used the right name, and had the right excuse. It was all too believable.

Using Nonverbal Communication in Phone Elicitation

Smiling creates happiness in your voice. According to Scharlemann, Eckel, Kacelnik, and Wilson (2001), we give and receive more trust by smiling. Indeed, even if the smile can't be seen, it can be felt. In their study "The Value of a Smile: Game Theory with a Human Face," they state: "Smiling increases trust among strangers. Subjects were more likely to trust photographs of smiling persons than unsmiling photographs of the same persons" (p. 13).

In addition to smiling, body posture; gestures; and voice tone, volume, speed, and pitch all affect how the person on the other end of the phone perceives us and our story. All these qualities are nonverbal communications that enhance our ability to influence our targets.

When I posed as a tech support representative during the three-stage attack, it was important that my voice's tone denoted authority rather than nervousness. Even though my target couldn't see my face, he or she could "hear" my smile, which contributed to building trust. My posture was one of authority too.

In stage three, when I was the employee calling tech support, for my pretext to be believable, my face had to show fear, and my voice's volume, pitch, and speed had to be slower and lower. My nonverbals had to say, "I'm sorry. I messed up. Please help me." Because I changed my facial expressions to match the emotion I was supposed to be showing, my pretext was stronger.

It is even said that how we sit and how we dress can affect our tone on the phone. In social-engineer.org newsletter #34 (http://www.social-engineer.org/newsletter/Social-Engineer.Org%20Newsletter%20Vol.%2003%20Iss.%2034.html), I discussed research into enclothed cognition conducted by researchers, Adam and Galinsky. Their research suggests that our perception of clothing affects how we handle certain tasks and approach a job we are asked to do.

This research further proves that our vocal tones and how we sound to our targets is affected by our clothing, our nonverbals, and much more. As mentioned previously, the same piece of clothing that was given a different "meaning" created a psychological bridge for the subjects to act a certain way. Knowing this means how I dress on engagement can and will influence the way I act.

I Am Not the Social Engineer You Are Looking For

Before phones and the Internet, scams were conducted in person. From Victor Lustig, who "sold" the Eiffel Tower a few times, to everyday street scams, in-person forms of social engineering have been used throughout history.

In recent years, story after story illustrates how criminals use impersonation to trick people into taking actions they shouldn't take. For example, in the United States, a man convinced a few of his buddies to rob a bank. Before the robbery, the man entered the bank, posing as a customer and an undercover federal agent. As his friends started to rob the bank, he stopped the crime, saving the day. He made "arrests" and took all the money as evidence. As he left with the criminals and bags of cash, employees felt the bank was safe and sound. But no police ever arrived to follow up.

Why do attacks like this work? With impersonation comes an inherent link to trust. When someone flashes a badge; wears the right uniform; and speaks, acts, and carries himself as the person he says he is, our minds get answers to unspoken questions:

- "Who is this person?"
- "What proof does he offer to back up his claims?"
- "Am I safe?"

All these questions get answered, and the target's mind is put at ease. This is the power of impersonation. In my introductory story about my warehouse job, I didn't need to vocalize those details, because my outfit said it all. I just needed to answer the leftover questions: "What do you want?" and "Why are you here?"

Once those questions were answered, my pretext did the rest of the work. In addition to physical impersonation, in person social engineering attacks allow for a wide array of vectors that can be hard with other forms of attack. For example, many firewalls and other technology stop attachments such as PDF and EXE files from entering email inboxes and being run. However, if these same files are instead contained on a USB stick, they can be installed on an employee's machine and run with less risk of being stopped.

Many times I've left lying around in a workplace a USB key or DVD labeled "Confidential," "Employee Bonus," or, unfortunately, "Private Pics" to pique the curiosity of the target. When he inserts the USB or DVD, his machine is compromised.

The infamous Stuxnet computer worm attack, as well as the more recent attempted attack on Dutch chemical company DSM, highlight how USB drops are still used. The element of curiosity can be dangerous when mixed with malicious software.

Using Nonverbal Communication in Impersonation

It may seem obvious that nonverbal communication is used in impersonation, but it is also crucial to understand. Because interaction is personal in impersonation attack methods, nonverbal communications affect the target the most.

It is natural to be nervous or scared when you fear being caught. If your pretext is one of authority, nerves and fear can ruin the nonverbal link that says, "I am sure of myself."

We will discuss this in greater detail in Chapter 8, which discusses the nonverbal side of elicitation. If the social engineer is showing expressions of anger, sadness, and fear, those same emotional states are mirrored in the target's brains.

Understanding how nonverbal communication can influence your targets makes it vital for social engineers not only to be able to recognize nonverbal signs but also to control the ones they display. For example, once we understand that having our hands in our pockets can be seen as a sign of weakness, we can either use that if our pretext is submissiveness or avoid doing that if our pretext is to be an authority figure.

Sometimes a social engineer can rely on nonverbal communication alone when performing impersonation. This is often the case with *tailgating*, in which someone who does not have access to a particular area gains access by following employees who do. Tailgating can be done in a few ways:

- **Employee smoking areas**: These areas, usually behind the building, often lack proper security so that employees can exit and enter easily. A social engineer can "join the tribe" of smokers and then try to walk back in with them.
- **Carrying a box or large object**: I cannot tell you how many times I have walked right into a building simply because I was carrying a box. As I approached the door, a helpful and kind employee saw me struggling and let me in. If a smaller, attractive female carries a heavy box, guys will fight over who will hold the door for her.
- **Fake badge**: Another successful method that even adds a layer of trust is a fake badge. The social engineer creates a realistic-looking badge that he knows will not give him access to the building. As he unsuccessfully swipes it a few times, helpful employees see him struggling and let him in.

These are just a few impersonation methods that do not involve speech much or at all, but do rely heavily on the social engineer's nonverbal communication skills. Everyone has internal radar that pings if something feels wrong, and that feeling is often based on how another person's nonverbal communication makes us feel. Knowing this solidifies the value of the social engineer's being able to control and utilize these signs to give off the right "feeling."

Using Social Engineering Skills

Social engineering skills don't always have to be used in a negative way; they also can be positive. I will briefly discuss this point to put into context how the rest of this book will progress. To reiterate, I define social engineering as any act that influences someone to perform an action that may or may not be in his or her best interest.

The Good

Positive social engineering is easy to understand. Suppose a child wants something from her parents. She approaches her mom and says, "Mommy, can I have the new Barbie doll?"

Mom says, "I don't know. Ask your father."

The girl approaches her dad sitting on the couch, cuddles up next to him, and says, "Mommy said I can get the new Barbie doll if you say it's okay. Can I, Daddy, pleeeease?"

"Of course, pumpkin," Dad says, looking down at those beautiful big eyes.

What just occurred? Without understanding psychology or nonverbal communication or communication modeling, the little girl employed all these techniques.

If I can speak from experience, the first request to Mom is usually made after a good deed or a moment of emotional closeness—a moment when trust and love hormones are heavy in the blood. But the real social engineering comes into play with Dad.

First is the power of touch. When the girl cuddles up and gets close to Dad, this creates an emotional bond. Then, by starting with the basic "Mom already said yes" approach, she applies social proof. Together these become an unstoppable force, and the little girl gets her wish.

Other, more serious examples may include rehab or therapy, where people are reframed and taught how to rethink their belief system. Once they reanalyze their beliefs, they can take a different path. In essence, they are influenced to take an action that may make them stop thinking negatively, stop abusing alcohol or drugs, or take another action that ends an abusive streak.

Social engineering can be used to influence someone to take an action that is good for her. It can be used to reframe her thinking, to create an atmosphere for growth, and to help change entrenched bad habits.

When one of my children was younger, he refused to eat breakfast. I saw this for what it was—a power play. He just wanted to be able to control this aspect of his life. It wasn't about defiance or being a bad kid. Knowing that it was all about his need to make a choice and be empowered by the ability to do so, I simply woke up one day and said,

"I know you're having a problem with breakfast before school, so it's up to you. Do you want cereal or eggs?"

He made a choice, he felt empowered, and in the end we both won. I was happy that my child ate, and my child was happy that he was empowered by choice. This type of social engineering is positive because the underlying principle is that both people win, there is no loser, and the change leaves everyone feeling better for having taken the action.

The Bad

The skills just mentioned also can be used by malicious social engineers. The main difference between the "good" and the "bad" is the intent. In the bad, the social engineer doesn't intend to help, change, or better your life—it's all about what he or she can gain.

On March 18, 1990, there was a knock at the side door of Boston's Gardner Museum. This door was to remain closed and not be opened, but the two men knocking were uniformed police officers. The security guard unlocked the door and let them in, only to find out they were not police at all. Using no weapons, they subdued the museum's two security guards, tied them up, and, in less than 90 minutes, stole 13 pieces of art worth $300 to $500 million.

This heist used the principles of influence and authority. We are taught to obey authority figures, especially the police. The thieves banked on that and banked over $300 million in art.

In the Antwerp diamond heist of 2003, Leonardo Notarbartolo rented space in an office building that housed a large diamond merchant for three years so that he could build credibility and rapport. He and his cohorts planned an attack posing as diamond merchants and breached a vault that was protected by multiple measures, cleaning out over $100 million worth of gems. Interestingly, they were caught when one of the five in the heist forgot to burn a bag of trash that contained evidence of the crime.

Hacking attacks such as those carried out against HBGary Federal, PBS's website, and Coca-Cola all started with a phishing email. Other operations, such as Night Dragon and Stuxnet, may have involved phone calls and specialized hardware. Each of these used or even focused on social engineering skills for success. Both sophisticated attacks against corporations and everyday scams such as grandparents being called and asked for money by someone purporting to be their grandchild involve the use of these skills. Both kinds of scams involve planning, information gathering, and heavy doses of nonverbal communication.

The Ugly

Yes, there is one step further than "the bad" when we discuss these skills. I won't cover this aspect in depth, because it is not my area of expertise. Recently I had a chance to interview ex-FBI agent and psychologist Mary Ellen O'Toole about how psychopaths utilize social engineering skills. She recalled some of the cases she has worked on and some she knows about that involved social engineering skills, with devastating effects. Consider Ted Bundy, who terrorized women for over four years in the 1970s and admitted to over 30 homicides. He utilized social engineering skills to carry out his crimes. Many of his attacks started with him pretexting as a police officer, using authority. His most effective method was pretending to be injured, using crutches or a fake cast, utilizing a plea for help and sympathy. His victims felt empathy for him and came to his aid. They were unfortunately repaid with death in most cases.

As I said, I don't want to dwell too long on this part, but it is important to mention that, when analyzed, each of these areas utilizes almost the same skill set. No matter if it is the good, the bad, or the ugly, social engineering looks the same, with one major difference: the intent.

Summary

To summarize, let me reiterate the definition of social engineering: "Any act that influences a person to take an action that may, or may not, be in their best interest." Seeing how nonverbal communications are used—whether through email, on the phone, or in person—cannot only enhance your abilities to communicate better, but it can help you stay safe.

Understanding that social engineering surrounds us each and every day and that it is part of all our communications is fun and exciting. It makes communicating an interesting learning experience.

As we move on to the next chapters, I want to say that this book is not meant to be an all-inclusive discussion of social engineering topics. It is meant to help you—the security professional, the teacher, the parent, the CEO, the therapist—enhance your understanding of the most commonly used nonverbals.

Each chapter will cover a portion of the body and the nonverbal communication it displays. The next chapter goes into one of the most communicative parts of the body: the hands. What do the hands say intentionally and unintentionally? How can you read the language of the hands? Finally, how can you use your hands to influence the emotional content of others?

All of these questions will be answered as we begin Chapter 3.

Decoding the Language of the Body

3

Understanding the Language of the Hands

As the tongue speaks to the ear, the gesture speaks to the eye.

—King James I

Humans are unique in how extensively and variably they communicate with their hands. Our hands are marvelous creations that can accomplish many things. Think back to when you were young and standing next to your parents and something scared you. You reached for their hands to receive comfort and protection.

Even before that time, your hands were the means through which you explored the world around you. As you got older, you learned how to use your hands to perform basic skills such as feeding and dressing yourself, to more advanced skills such as painting, sculpting, cooking, and manipulating tools. A surgeon spends hundreds of hours training his or her hands to react in tiny movements to save lives. A musician learns finger placement, keystrokes, and more. In his 1980 book *Hands*, John Napier made an interesting point. He said that we explore the world around us using our eyes and hands, but only one of these permits us to see around corners and in the dark. He also stated that humans are the only creatures to communicate meaningfully with their hands. Regardless of how skilled a speaker you become, you will still use your hands to augment your speech.

This is my focus for this chapter: how our hands communicate not only language but also emotions to those we interact with. Napier went on to say that the hands mirror the brain, because what the brain feels is shown not only in the face but also in the hands.

There is a direct connection between the emotions we feel and how our hands move. In 1973 Dr. Paul Ekman and Dr. Wallace Friesen conducted research that solidified this thought. In a paper they produced called "Hand Movements," they broke down the different ways in which emotions are shown with the hands. Using their research, along with research that came in its wake, I will show you how important it is to understand, watch, and decipher these important signals.

Communicating with Your Hands

This section does not discuss sign language—probably the first thing that springs to mind when you think of communicating with your hands. Although it is fascinating to read the studies that link the brain and that form of communication, my focus is to understand how people leak emotional content using their hands.

Suppose you walk into your living room and see cookie crumbs on the floor. You always tell your son not to eat cookies before dinner, but there is the evidence on the floor and on his face. You do the typical parent thing and ask, "Where did all these crumbs come from?" As your son decides whether to lie, try to picture what his hands are doing.

Or maybe remember the time you had to get in front of your high school class to read a paper or poem you wrote. When your name was called, you walked to the front of the room. As your shaking hands held the paper, your classmates looked either amused at your pain or ready to mock you after class. What were your hands doing?

Think back to a time when you were about to interview for a job. You pumped yourself up to be confident; you knew you were qualified for this job, and you needed it. You went in calm and ready for every question. You answered each question with confidence. Then the interviewer asked if you had experience in something you'd never heard of. You needed to decide whether to make up an answer or admit you had no knowledge of the topic. What were your hands doing?

Finally, think back to videos you have seen of police interviews. The suspect sits there with a smug look on his face. Maybe his hands tap the table as he waits impatiently. The officer starts the interview with a leading question: "When you were at the Lazy Tree Bar on June the first, did you see Rico there with his girlfriend?"

"No!" the suspect exclaims. "I told you already I didn't see him there that night!" as he slams a closed fist on the table.

"Oh, so you *were* at that bar, then. I thought you said earlier you weren't even there that night." the detective says, shrugging his shoulders and pointing at the suspect with one finger.

As the look of "Uh oh" comes over his face, what are his hands doing?

In each of these scenarios, an emblem, gesture, illustrator, or manipulator was displayed. In the final interrogation scene, you might have pictured the suspect rubbing his hands together in stress, or playing with a ring or piece of clothing. What is the difference among these, and what emotions do they reveal?

In the Ekman and Wallace study mentioned previously, the researchers discussed how we display emotion in our hands by using emblems, gestures, illustrators, and manipulators. Each of these can be used to determine the emotional state and the true message that is being sent.

Learning to discern, decipher, and use this form of nonverbal communication is essential to discuss in the context of normal communications and also as a social engineer. In this study, Dr. Ekman referenced a work from Dr. David Efron, who, in 1941, conducted a fascinating and still widely used study, entitled "Gestures and Environment," on nonverbal communication. Studying two groups of people who immigrated to New York from different countries, he found that there was a definite cultural influence to emblems and body language that was learned from the culture and passed down.

Using Efron's research, Ekman and Wallace developed a system of understanding this form of body language. They broke the system into three parts: origin, coding, and usage.

Origin

The *origin* of a nonverbal behavior is how the behavior became a part of someone's communication style. Ekman and Wallace divided the origin into three different categories: those that are built into the nervous system; survival instincts; and those that vary with culture, class, family, or the individual.

Understanding the origin of a nonverbal behavior means we will judge or view nonverbal hand emblems based not on our own experiences or origin, but on the person's origin.

Coding

Coding is the relationship between the act and its meaning. Whether the emblem looks like the act can determine the type of coding involved.

Dr. Ekman explains that an arbitrarily coded emblem has no visual resemblance to its significance. As an example, one of the most widely used hand gestures, known commonly as "flipping someone the bird," does not physically or physiologically represent either a bird or the act that gesture stands for, does it?

On the other hand, an *iconically coded* emblem carries a clue to its decoding in its appearance. In other words, it looks like what is being said. For example, making the shape of a pistol with your thumb and forefinger. That emblem looks like a pistol and is clearly understood.

Finally, an *intrinsically coded* emblem is similar to an iconically coded emblem. It looks like the act being signified, but instead of just resembling the emblem, it acts out the coding. For example, I am from a demonstrative family. It's not uncommon, when we joke around, for us to make a fist and lightly hit each other. An intrinsically coded emblem is not just a clenched fist but the act of actually hitting another person in jest.

Usage

Usage is just like it sounds: When is the nonverbal hand movement used? The external conditions found when the act is used, the supporting verbal behavior, what information is being relayed, and whether it is interactive or communicative all play a part in determining the usage.

Combining the origin, coding, and usage helped Ekman and Wallace create different aspects of nonverbal communication with the hands. Understanding each can help us see what someone is trying to say or what emotion is being portrayed.

The following sections discuss three aspects of this nonverbal communication of the hands: emblems, gestures/illustrators, and manipulators.

Emblems

As I mentioned in the first chapter, Dr. Ekman defines an emblem as a nonverbal communication of the hands that has five aspects:

- A direct verbal translation consisting of a short phrase or a word or two
- A precise meaning that is known by a group, class, or subculture

- Most often deliberately used with the conscious intent to send another person a particular message
- The receiver knows that the emblem was sent to him or her deliberately.
- The sender takes responsibility for having made the communication.

Just as people are aware of the words they speak, most are aware of the emblems they use. In addition, just like we have slips of the tongue, "emblem slips" can occur, but for the most part the sender is very aware of the emblems being used.

Understanding the origin can help the social engineer understand the emotional state of what the person is saying or not saying based on understanding emblems.

This can sometimes have serious implications. What you see in Figure 3-1 is often thought of as "I love you," but in certain areas it could be interpreted as a sign for a gang called the Latin Kings. You would want to be cautious with using this gesture in certain areas.

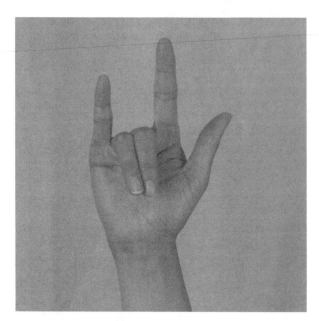

Figure 3-1: "I love you" or a gang sign?

The next figures show a few more examples to prove the point.

In the U.S. the hand emblem shown in Figure 3-2 says, "Stop what you're doing!" If used by an authority figure, it is a commanding emblem that says to cease and stay put until further notice. Yet in Malaysia this hand sign summons a waiter.

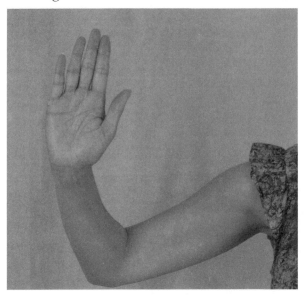

Figure 3-2: "Come here" or "Go away"?

In the U.S. the sign shown in Figure 3-3 says, "Come here." In Japan it is considered rude to use this sign. In Singapore it represents death.

The emblem shown in Figure 3-4 stands for "Good luck"—unless you are Italian or Turkish. To them it represents the female genitalia. In Asia it is also considered a very obscene gesture.

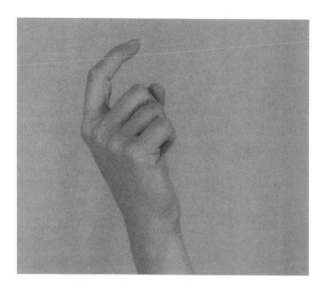

Figure 3-3: "Come here" or seduction or death?

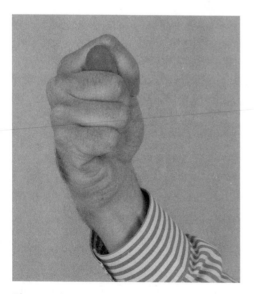

Figure 3-4: "Good luck" or an obscene gesture?

These are just a few of the dozens of emblems. Each has a direct verbal translation, is precise in what that translation is, and is often deliberately used. The receiver knows the message is for him or her, and the sender meant to send it. That by definition is an emblem.

In each of these examples, understanding not only the emblem but also the origin can alter our understanding of the person's emotional state. In addition, we can alter the person's emotional state, either intentionally or by mistake, by using emblems that are unique to his or her origin.

Although emblems can be displayed in many places on the body, they generally involve the hands primarily, and then the head, face, and posture.

Illustrators

In "Hand Movements," Dr. Ekman stated that "Illustrators are those acts which are intimately related on a moment-to-moment basis with speech, with phrasing, content, voice contours, loudness, etc." In other words, illustrators are gestures that augment what is being said. They are somewhat similar to emblems because they are used with awareness and intent, although illustrators usually are used peripherally.

Here are some of the factors that make illustrators different from emblems:

- They usually do not have a precise verbal definition.
- They usually never occur without conversation.
- They are shown only by the speaker, not the listener.

Illustrators can change based on the mood, problems, or attitude of the person using them. They are generally used more when a person is feeling awkward in speech or thought.

Sudden changes in the type or frequency of illustrators can often hint at deception or a significant change in baselines, telling the social engineer to pay better attention to the person.

Illustrators are broken into eight categories or types:

- Batons are movements that emphasize a particular word or phrase.
- Ideographs are movements that sketch the path of a thought.
- Deictic movements point to an object, place, or event.
- Rhythmic movements depict the pacing of the event.
- Spatial movements depict a spatial relationship.
- Kinetographs are movements that depict a bodily action or a non-human physical action.
- Pictographs are movements that draw a picture in the air of the shape being referred to.
- Emblematic movements are used to illustrate a statement, even replacing a word or phrase.

Illustrators are interesting to watch for and can help the social engineer determine a baseline and figure out how the person thinks and reacts to emotional triggers.

In his book *Telling Lies*, Dr. Ekman relates a very interesting fact with regard to illustrators: "Illustrators increase with involvement with what is being said. People tend to illustrate more than usual when they are furious, horrified, very agitated, distressed, or excitedly enthused" (106).

He subsequently explains and gives a few reasons why people may stop illustrating. Emotional investment, boredom, and feigning concern can all be reasons why someone would stop using illustrators. In addition, Dr. Ekman states that those who would employ deceit, if not skilled or practiced at their lie, may stop using illustrators because they are cognating what to say and not how to describe it properly.

All of these signs point to the skilled social engineer watching for their subject's baselines and any alterations to that baseline during the conversation.

Manipulators

A manipulator is defined as any movement that involves a manipulation or grooming of a body part or article of clothing. Generally it is caused by nervousness, discomfort, habit, or a need to relax. One important point I need to bring up is that just because you notice a person is utilizing manipulators, do *not* automatically assume this proves deception.

Instead, looking for manipulators is a good way to notice a change in someone's baseline. You should ask yourself how they acted before the conversation got to this emotional level. Noticing their baseline can help the social engineer see indications (again, not deception) of changes to the emotions of that person.

Examples of manipulators are people who play with their hair, hands, or rings. Or maybe they are always adjusting their cuffs, buttons, or other clothing. These indicators can be used to determine if the person is either comforting himself or if he is nervous.

Figures 3-5 through 3-7 show examples of common manipulators you may notice.

Figure 3-5: Hand wringing is a common manipulator.

When someone is nervous or unsure, they may wring their hands. Let's say that Ben's baseline was hand steepling, discussed later this chapter, showing confidence. Then I started to question him on his whereabouts the other night, and he starts to do what you see in Figure 3-5. That change in the baseline can indicate that something about that question or the thoughts the question brought up made him nervous.

A good social engineer will decide if this is an area to explore more or to leave alone, all depending on the desired emotional level.

Figure 3-6: Another one is playing with some form of jewelry.

Another nervous hand gesture to watch for is if someone starts to play with their jewelry or even buttons and other articles of clothing. Sometimes people play with clothing or jewelry as a pacifier. Maybe the person that gave them that item is a close friend or family member and when they feel uncomfortable they begin to manipulate this article of clothing and it makes them feel less nervous. Again, a great manipulator to watch for during a conversation.

In Figure 3-7, notice another such set of manipulators. If Selena were standing with her arms at her side as a baseline then during the conversation you see her fold her one arm under her breasts and across her stomach while starting to play with her jewelry, this is a good indication of an emotional change. The arm placement may indicate discomfort and the jewelry playing mixed with her facial expression can tell us she is contemplating something, and it isn't truly comfortable for her.

In *Telling Lies*, Dr. Ekman discusses these important parts of nonverbal language: "Manipulators are on the edge of consciousness" (110). This means that even though a person knows what he is doing, he is reacting to a subconscious trigger to begin the manipulation. This is where watching for the baseline and any changes to the baseline can make a huge difference in understanding changes to emotional content during a conversation.

Figure 3-7: Another example of a nervous gesture

Noticing these signs can give the social engineer a leg up in engagements. It also can help determine if your actions or line of questions are causing the person discomfort.

High-Confidence Hand Displays

As I mentioned, the hands are amazing tools and amazing communicators. They also can indicate when a person is feeling confident. Knowing this is powerful for the social engineer. People enjoy being told good things about themselves, appealing to their egos. A confident person can be influenced using proper ego appeals, which can build rapport fast. The person wants to maintain that feeling at all costs—even giving up valuable information.

The next section goes through a few hand displays that can indicate the person is feeling confident about his or her position. Once you learn to see these quickly and clearly, you will be able to adjust your approaches and opening lines to match the communication style of your subjects. This will allow you to communicate with them in the way they want to be communicated with.

The Steeple

This hand movement occurs when the person creates a steeple with his finger. This can be done with one finger (usually the pointer) on both hands or with the whole hand, as shown in Figures 3-8 and 3-9.

Figure 3-8: The one-finger steeple

In Figure 3-9, not only is Ben steepling but he is also looking pretty confident, which is when you normally see people steepling.

Figure 3-10 shows Jordan Harbinger. Through his company, The Art of Charm, Jordan teaches men to have more confidence and to accomplish certain goals. His stance in Figure 3-10 says, "I am confident, I am powerful, and you should listen to me."

Not only does Jordan have a high-confidence steeple going on here, but his leaning forward posture says he is ready to take charge, and his head tilt says he is trusting. The lean-in is important to notice. If done too aggressively it can show anger or impatience, but a slight lean in can show some increased interest and even help elicitation more. Jordan nailed it here and his slight lean-in, steeple, and head tilt all show interest and confidence at the same time. There is a lot in this photo that commands the respect Jordan is trying to sell here.

Figure 3-9: The whole-hand steeple

Figure 3-10: What image does he want to portray?

In some cases, steepling is used as a territorial display, basically saying, "I am confident in what I am saying despite your challenge." Notice in Figure 3-11 how master weatherman Bernie Rayno displays this hand movement during one particularly pressing interview.

Figure 3-11: Bernie Rayno saying he knows what he's talking about

What was particularly interesting about this interview was that the more Rayno was pressed into a corner and challenged, the higher he displayed his steeple. Bernie was being interviewed about potential damaging radiation hitting America from the damage related to the tsunami in Japan. His interviewer was pressing him into a corner and being very aggressive. The more aggressive she got, the higher his steeple was. At one point he was steepling as high as eye level, as seen in Figure 3-12. Often when territory is being threatened or when confidence is great, we can see steeples going higher and higher until the hands are behind the head with the arms out, as shown in Figure 3-13.

Figure 3-12: The more aggressive his interviewer became the higher was his steeple.

Eventually the territorial display will be high enough that it will take on the form of what you see in Figure 3-13.

Figure 3-13: A high confidence territorial display

Imagine that Ben is feeling very confident about an answer he just gave to a pressing question. His confidence during his answer might have been joined with a steeple; after his answer you might see that steeple end in what is shown in Figure 3-13. Ben is not only feeling confident here, but he is sure enough to let everyone else around him know that too. This display can be followed by a very confident reflective look as the person focuses on their own thoughts.

Thumb Displays

Thumbs are often displayed when a person feels important, confident, sure of themself or wants everyone around him or her to feel reassured. Sometimes thumbs are shown when someone is feeling confident or wants to display high confidence. We can see examples of this in photos taken of businesspeople, leaders, or other important people, as shown in Figure 3-14.

Figure 3-14: Using the thumbs in this manner can suggest high confidence or that what a person is saying is important.

Ventral Displays

The anatomical term *ventral* refers to the parts of the body oriented toward the abdomen—for instance, the insides of the arms and legs. Exposing these ventral areas in an open fashion indicates that you are trustworthy and easy to deal with.

The hands can command, demand, or openly invite. In reviewing pictures of past leaders in the U.S., I found that former President Bill Clinton used open-hand displays. As shown in Figure 3-15, open-hand displays invite the person to become part of your tribe and to feel comfortable with what you are proposing. When mixed with other powerful nonverbals such as head tilts and smiles (which are discussed later in this book), they are a force to be reckoned with.

The opposite of an open ventral display, as shown in Figure 3-16, is the closed-hand display, which is demanding and not open at all.

We generally see this display when someone is commanding others, or telling them what to do—often when people are being scolded—and, in general, other body language that accompanies this type of display is tight and more aggressive.

Other open displays are things like wearing shirts with the cuffs rolled up, or women with their hands on their hips. These are similar in saying, "I am open to you, so open up to me." If you want to build trust and rapport with people fast, this nonverbal is one to practice.

Figure 3-15: "Please come with me."

Figure 3-16: "You will do what I say."

Genital Framing

The last high-confidence hand display we will discuss is called *genital framing*. In essence this nonverbal states, "I am a virile young man. Look, here's proof." The person hooks his thumbs into his belt loops or pockets, and his fingers "frame" or point to his genitals. Figure 3-17 shows the normal stance that accompanies this nonverbal.

Figure 3-17: "Look at me; I'm a strong man."

This nonverbal shows confidence and is a display of dominance. You might not believe this display is still used outside of old Westerns or *Happy Days* reruns. But now that you know about it, you will notice it more than you thought.

Low-Confidence and Stress Hand Displays

Just as the hands can tell you if your subject is feeling good, happy, or positive, they also can tell you if your subject is feeling low or stressed. The following sections cover a few of the many tells that you may notice in people that give you a clearer picture of their emotional state.

Hand Wringing or Rubbing

When someone is nervous or uncomfortable, she may clasp her hands tightly, creating a "white knuckle effect," as shown in Figure 3-5. Other times she may wring her hands or rub them together. You can also observe discomfort from manipulation of rings or other jewelry (refer back to Figures 3-5 through 3-7). Other signs can be constant knuckle cracking or using the hands to scratch, rub, or manipulate clothing or other parts of the body. All these signs point to a negative emotional state in the person.

Thumb Displays

Just as a thumbs up means all is good, a thumbs-down display means all is bad, as shown in Figure 3-18. In addition, whereas high thumbs can indicate confidence, low thumbs or hidden thumbs can indicate a lack of confidence and comfort. Notice in Figure 3-19 how the hands might appear to be steepling (a high-confidence movement), but hidden thumbs indicate something totally different.

Figure 3-18: Thumbs down for this performance

Although Figure 3-19 is a steeple, it is a very low confidence steeple because the thumbs are hidden.

Figure 3-19: Hidden thumbs can point to low confidence.

Closed for Confidence

As stated previously, the hands indicate a lot about the person's emotional state. Whereas high hand signs all point to high confidence, take special notice if the person's hands display closed nonverbal signals.

Maybe the person is standing with his hands behind his back or in his pockets, as shown in Figure 3-20. Watch for other indicators, and see if this display can point to a lack of confidence.

Although Ben has a confident stance here, hiding his hands can indicate he might not be feeling as strong as he is trying to portray.

Some other key hand movements to watch for are involved in the way someone may point at another person. Pointing in a quick jabbing motion can indicate impatience, emphasis, or even anger. Whereas pointing with the palm up and the fingers extended can build rapport and reinforce positive feelings in the person you are talking to.

Figure 3-20: Hiding hands can indicate low confidence.

Getting a Handle on the Hands

As you can probably tell, this is a huge amount of information to process, so how can you possibly master it and use it? Practice makes perfect. Maybe more accurately, someone I know in SEAL Team Six will say, "Perfect practice makes perfect." We don't want to practice the wrong things and reinforce bad habits. The more you observe, the more you educate yourself on the meanings of these cues, and the more you practice perfectly, the easier it will become to pick up on these little cues.

The next step, once you train yourself to notice these signs, is to teach yourself how to use them. If you walked into an office and you saw the scene shown in Figure 3-21, what would you assume? Take a minute to study the picture.

Figure 3-21: What do you see here?

Did you notice that Ben is trying to assert his dominance? What do Selena's hands indicate?

She doesn't look too comfortable with his approach, does she? If you saw this scene and, as a social engineer, you wanted to win Selena's rapport and trust quickly, what action would you take?

You don't want to alienate Ben, but you want to show that you see Selena's discomfort and are there to help, without making her more uncomfortable.

By disengaging the man in his genital framing and engaging them both in positive dialog, you can accomplish your goal. Use high-confidence but non-territorial hand displays, such as open-hand displays and high-thumb displays.

If you were to come in and start to frame around Selena or act territorial you would basically start a territory war with Ben. This builds rather than reduces tension. By utilizing high-confidence displays that are open and nonaggressive, you can diffuse the situation and win rapport and trust from both parties.

Using this type of information in your approach can mean the difference between success or failure during your engagements.

Summary

As I mentioned above, there is a lot of information in these pages. It can be hard to try and master it all at one time. My suggestion is to not go into any engagement looking for hand, arm, thumb, and genital framing displays. Take some time to notice this in "the wild," as I say. Go to a mall and watch two people talking in the distance; hit a pub and watch a guy trying to pick up a girl, then a guy getting rejected. You will be amazed at what you see.

Also you can watch the news, interviews or talk shows to see a lot of this in action too.

Remember, your goal is not to pick up on every little movement and try to decipher exactly what is being said, but rather to look for changes in these baselines and decipher the emotional changes during your interactions. Notice if someone appears to be confident, then adjust your approach to be fitting. Notice if the person seems to be timid and shy, then adjust your approach to be more mild and quiet.

Learn to adapt your approaches and your nonverbal hand displays to fit with the "tribe" you are trying to get in with. Doing this will enhance your ability as a social engineer and make you an amazing communicator.

All of this and we have only touched on the hands! In the next chapter we start to move down the body to discuss the torso, legs, and feet.

4

The Torso, Legs, and Feet

The language of the body is the key that can unlock the soul.

—Konstantin Stanislavsky

The preceding chapter touched on how the hands can communicate feelings. The hands can be so descriptive and engaging that they can tell a whole story without your ever having to speak. But what about the lower half of the body? Is it as telling? Are key indicators of a person's emotional state buried deep in the torso, legs, and feet?

The legs and feet are a means of transportation. They take us places, help carry heavy loads, and keep our bodies balanced. At the same time, the legs and especially the feet can be a source of sensual pleasure and extreme sensitivity.

The limbic system, which controls our nonverbal behavior, keeps the lower half of our body honest. Because the hands and arms are in front of us, we notice what we are doing, but with the legs and feet, we often don't. This means that leg, foot, and torso movements often can be keys in determining the true emotions of the person you are dealing with. Let me start with the legs and feet and work up.

Legs and Feet

The legs and feet can tell us if someone is feeling happy, sad, nervous, uncomfortable, or even territorial. Learning to pick up on these indicators can help you read your subjects and understand their frame of mind. You may have seen the film *Happy Feet*, about a dancing penguin. He was happiest when he was dancing.

That is not too far from reality. When someone is happy, he may bounce on the balls of his feet or rock on his heels, or his toes may point up. Robin Dreeke calls these "gravity-defying gestures." Figure 4-1 shows a gravity-defying toe lift.

Figure 4-1: Gravity-defying gestures like this raised toe indicate happiness.

It is important not to confuse these gravity-defying gestures with being jittery. People might bounce or rock on their feet a lot out of habit or due to discomfort—that would be noteworthy in determining their baseline behavior. How can you determine which it is? Look for sudden changes during the conversation. If someone is bouncing but suddenly stops when asked a question, this can indicate a change in his or her comfort level—in baseline.

In one instance with my son, who has jittery legs, I decided to try to find out the truth about a situation with his friends. I asked him to sit down with me in the living room. As if on cue, his foot started bouncing. I asked him how things were going with his friends. "Good," he replied. I saw I would have to dig deeper, so after a few mundane questions I asked, "What is the situation between this person and this person?" His foot stopped moving, and he placed it firmly on the floor, pointing toward the door (another indicator I will discuss in a moment). Did this sudden shift mean that my son was about to lie to or deceive me? No. It meant that he went from feeling comfortable to feeling uncomfortable. This in turn meant that whatever was going on with his friends was directly affecting him. I eventually found out that a situation between two guys in his group was affecting his friendships and upsetting him.

What did the foot plant and point mean? Our feet point in the direction we are going. Have you ever tried to walk straight ahead with your feet pointing inward or outward? Our feet and legs point not only in the direction we are heading, but also in the direction we *want* to head. You can see this often in conversations where one of the parties no longer wants to be there. Before he excuses himself, you can see his feet and legs shift away from the other party or group. Figure 4-2 shows an example of leg direction.

Figure 4-2: Who's interested in whom? Look at the legs to decide.

Not only does the direction of the legs and feet indicate whether the person is staying or going, but it also can show interest or disinterest. Much emphasis is placed on the face, especially when it comes to dating. Often, in a dating scenario, one party might show polite facial expressions, even as his or her legs and feet indicate the actual interest level.

For instance, a man may approach a woman who gives a warm smile, but as he approaches, her legs and feet point away from him, or were never moved to point toward him, indicating that her interest lies elsewhere. As a social engineer, it is important to try to pick up on these cues to determine if you have built enough rapport to keep the target's interest.

Our feet and legs also are used in territorial displays. If you engage with a target and you notice him beginning to widen his stance, this is a good indicator that he might be feeling threatened and might be trying to establish dominance over his territory. The image on the left in Figure 4-3 shows how things may look when the conversation is going well. Notice that Selena's and Ben's legs are close together and their feet are pointed toward each other. If something is said that changes that, or if the person becomes agitated or defensive, you may see what is pictured on the right. Selena's legs have taken a wider, more territorial stance, and her feet are no longer pointing toward Ben in interest.

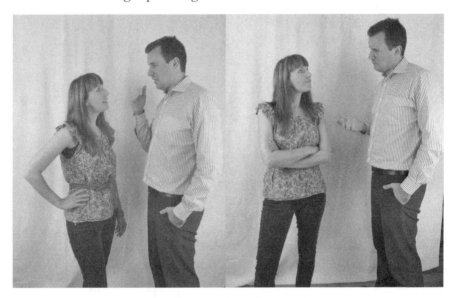

Figure 4-3: From comfort (left) to discomfort (right)

One final display I want to talk about is leg crossing. The way we cross or do not cross our legs can say much about our feelings of comfort or discomfort. If you remember when I spoke about the hands, I talked about how open gestures indicate trust and warmth, making the target trust you. Legs have similar power in that they can indicate whether we are happy, open, and warm or are putting up barriers due to discomfort.

For instance, a target sitting as shown in Figure 4-4 indicates high confidence. This comfortable, relaxed pose offers no barrier, saying, "I feel good."

Figure 4-4: "I feel confident in what I am saying."

On the other hand, crossing our legs while also pointing them even slightly away from the other person can be a way to create some distance—a barrier of sorts. Figure 4-5 shows this type of leg stance. How do you feel looking at this image? Is she open and friendly or closed and cold?

We decide whether we will like or trust someone very quickly, and our nonverbal behavior mirrors those feelings. We cross our legs politely toward people we favor, but we use leg crossing as shown in Figure 4-5 as a barrier for those we do not like.

Figure 4-5: Is she friendly or not?

Our legs and feet hold a wealth of nonverbal communications. As we move up the body, there are even more. The next section discusses the torso and arms.

Torso and Arms

Suppose you are in a packed subway car in which the only spot left is right next to you. In comes a man who looks like he has skipped a few baths. As he gets closer, you can smell that is certainly the case. What do you do? You can't go anywhere. You may at first turn your head, and then you find yourself leaning away. The few centimeters of distance won't affect the odor assaulting your olfactory senses, but you still try to get away. Why?

We tend to lean away from things we do not like and lean into things we do like. Now remove the dirty, smelly man from that scene and replace him with a beautiful person of the opposite sex who has just bathed. Which way are you leaning now?

Subconsciously, the leaning of our torso can tell us who we favor in a group. Grab a picture of yourself and a group of friends. Since you know who is emotionally closer to whom, see if you can notice torso leaning that supports that knowledge.

Take a look at Figure 4-6, and see how clear it is who likes whom.

Figure 4-6: Who does Ben really like?

In Figure 4-6, both women are leaning toward Ben, but Ben is leaning more toward Selena, indicating that is where his interest truly lies.

Even when the target is seated, the torso can tell us what he or she is thinking. Take a look at Figure 4-7, and decide whether Selena is comfortable or wants to leave.

If you think Selena wants to leave, you are correct. A shift in the torso, maybe toward the front as in Figure 4-7, indicates that Selena wants to leave.

The key with the torso is to watch for the lean. Where and how the target leans can tell you who she likes and who she doesn't, as well as whether she is comfortable versus wanting to leave. These indicators can help you adapt, adjust, and answer appropriately.

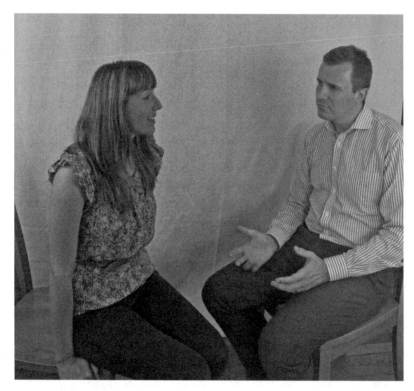

Figure 4-7: Will you stay or will you go?

Remember, if you see a person leaning toward another, that may indicate interest or comfort, whereas leaning away means discomfort or lack of interest. That simple tell can help a social engineer in a few ways. First, if the person you are dealing with leans away from you, you're coming on too strong.

One engagement I was on, I wanted to get some information from a couple sitting on the couch in a hotel. I approached them full head on, all 6 feet 3 inches of me looming over them and leaning into the man to ask my question. What I saw told me I just blew any chance I had: He leaned so far back that he almost pushed his body through the couch. Obviously his interest was in getting away from me.

Another way is to indicate your interest after rapport. When the person you are talking to starts to express their feelings or thoughts, leaning in slightly gives the impression you are interested and listening to what they are saying. This shows that you trust them and want to hear what they say, and that goes a long way toward building and maintaining rapport.

Think about animals that are about to fight. A gorilla, for instance, may puff out its chest as a way of saying, "I'm big, and you don't want to mess with me." Doing so also helps the gorilla take in more oxygen to prepare its body for a potential altercation. Humans are no different. When a person is feeling territorial, his or her chest puffs out.

Another clear sign to watch for is heaving of the chest. Heaving or heavy breathing results in taking in more oxygen, which indicates discomfort at some level, whereas a large exhale followed by dropping of the shoulders may indicate sadness or resignation.

What about the arms? Are they simply an extension of the hands and, as such, communicate the same things? The interesting thing about the arms is that they bridge the gap between the torso and hands. They link some of the nonverbal communications from both the torso and the hands.

Take a look at Figures 4-8 and 4-9 and decide which person you would want to approach.

Figure 4-8: This very open display denotes warmth and friendliness.

Figure 4-9: This arm display, mixed with the other body language, says "I am not too open to your ideas."

In Figure 4-9, it is not difficult to intuit that crossed arms are being used to create a barrier between the woman and someone else. Note, however, that crossed arms don't always indicate a barrier. The person might be cold or might simply be comfortable in a crossed-arm position; other signs must help indicate this emotional level. In Figure 4-9, the torso and leg positions indicate a level of disinterest. Another key indicator is where the arms are crossed. Arms crossed high on the stomach and under the breasts indicates discomfort. This type of arm-cross display is protective, in essence saying, "I am uncomfortable."

It is important to note that crossed arms alone do not indicate disinterest or discomfort. As with most other body language signs, look for sudden changes to the baseline to help indicate emotional level.

Figure 4-8, on the other hand, shows open ventral displays (described in Chapter 3). The sensitive or front part of the arms is exposed, in essence saying, "I am comfortable with you; I trust you." If you see the displays shown in Figure 4-8, you can assume you have built rapport.

Besides indicating comfort, ventral displays can indicate confidence. Figure 4-10 shows how ventral displays can be used to claim territory. If not kept in check, this display can seem disrespectful or arrogant.

Figure 4-10: When Ben sits this way, he is claiming his territory, but the open ventrals are disrespectful.

In Figure 4-10, Ben is leaning back in his chair with his legs open—a ventral display. His torso lean and arm position can be taken as a lack of respect and claiming territory that may not be his to claim.

Another arm display that many parents often see is the shrug. When mixed with words, what does a nonverbal like the one shown in Figure 4-11 mean?

Figure 4-11: The all-too-familiar shrug

What is interesting about this particular nonverbal is not just seeing it when someone is saying "I don't know," but seeing it when the verbals don't match this sign. I'll give an example to illustrate what I mean.

If you watch interviews, talk shows, presidential debates, or other live events, you may see this behavior. You are observing someone making a speech about something they believe in, perhaps as part of a political campaign.

A question or argument is raised that causes a pause of a second or two. As the candidate starts to answer, his head is nodding "yes," but you see what is shown in Figure 4-11. Even a slight shoulder shrug can indicate that a person is unsure of what they are saying. The head nod says "yes," but the body language says "I'm not sure."

Even more powerful to watch for is the single shoulder shrug. Many consider this to be a nonverbal contradiction. As in, I want to say yes, but my brain is saying no or I don't know. The single shrug is often unconscious and something to watch for.

Summary

The torso and arms convey a wealth of information. To summarize, look for the lean in the torso. A lean forward or back, toward you or away can indicate interest or comfort level.

The arms are similar. Look for signs of comfort or discomfort. Do the arms show you that the target is closed off, creating a barrier that might indicate he feels threatened? Or are the arms wide open, indicating rapport building and comfort?

Also look for signs of calm breathing or tense, deep breaths. This can help you see if your target is feeling threatened or even angry rather than calm and collected.

Our goal as social engineers is to create a calm, relaxed environment that puts the target at ease. When you see that the nonverbals match, you know you are on the path to success.

To truly see these signs, you need to focus on one last part of the body: the face, which is the subject of the next chapter.

5

The Science Behind the Face

If you want to know what someone is feeling you must watch for the temporary changes in the face.

—Dr. Paul Ekman, Unmasking the Face

O ver the past 45 years, Dr. Ekman's research has helped the world realize how vital the face is in reading emotions, and numerous other researchers have carried this torch forward. The face is so important that this book's longest chapter is devoted to it.

This chapter doesn't merely reiterate existing research; rather, it takes that research into an area on which it hasn't yet focused: social engineering.

It's said that the eyes are the windows to the soul. If that is true, the face reflects your emotional content. In fact, Dr. Ekman notes that the face is the primary—and the clearest—channel of emotion. Learning to read and react to this emotional content, decide what tactic to use, and choose when to apply your own emotion will give you seemingly superhuman abilities.

In one engagement, I began by building rapport with my target. The conversation was going great, and elicitation was working. I wanted to take the vector, or plan of attack, one step further and really enter the guy's "tribe" by mirroring some of his emotions about his coworkers who had just left. I turned to him and said, "I'm sorry; I should have introduced myself. My name is Paul—Paul Williams." I extended my hand. He shook it and answered, "It's okay; I'm just as rude. Greg Hurly."

I continued, "Those two who just left, do you work with them?"

"Yeah. The guy, Roger—he and I work for Sarah." Greg let out an audible sigh, but even more telling was his expression, similar to the one shown in Figure 5-1.

Figure 5-1: What do you see here?

When you look at this photo, what do you see? Some see arrogance or smugness. Both are good guesses. I see contempt.

Recognizing this expression allowed me to extend myself into Greg's tribe even more. I also sensed he had some problems dealing with his female boss. "So, Greg, maybe you can help me. I have a pretty rough female boss too. How do you deal with it? Maybe you can give me some pointers."

For the next 25 minutes Greg poured out his life to me. From then on, if I needed anything, I just had to ask. Being able to read Greg's facial expression enabled me to alter my communication to be more fitting to him. I built rapport, established trust, and gained the information I needed to succeed.

This chapter will help you learn how to do these things. It incorporates research from scientists such as Dr. Ekman, Dr. Wallace V. Friesen, and Dr. Maureen O'Sullivan, as well as practitioners such as Paul Kelly, a former Secret Service agent and known "truth wizard" identified in Dr. Ekman's & Dr. O'Sullivan's research on evaluating truthfulness. You will learn how to read the emotional content of someone's face and then alter your communication to fit.

Just the FACS

After spending many years researching facial expressions, Dr. Ekman teamed up with Dr. Friesen in the 1980s. They created a system that mapped the muscular movements of the face and classified them into action units (AUs). They believed that by learning to identify which muscles are used to create a facial expression, we can begin to see smaller "tells" of emotional content.

After more than 30 years of use, the Facial Action Coding System (FACS) has become a standard in this area of study.

The AUs are to be learned in groups. The groups are based upon the location and/or type of action involved. First, the AUs in the upper face are taught, which affect the eyebrows, forehead, and eyelids. Then, the lower face AUs are presented in five groups: up/down, horizontal, oblique, orbital, and miscellaneous actions. After learning each group, you practice scoring facial behavior.

FACS explains each AU with three main ideas:

- Appearance Changes
- How to reproduce the AU
- Score the intensity of the AU

Each muscular movement is broken down into an AU that describes what muscles are activated to create that expression. Ekman's work into emotional studies tells you when these emotions are triggered and what can trigger them. Combining these two aspects helps us to understand facial expressions as an equation.

If emotion is triggered by stimuli, neurons will fire, sending electrical impulses to the face, moving muscles in reaction, and showing this emotion externally.

Stimuli + Emotion = Muscular Triggers.

I won't go much deeper into the FACS system here, as you can get a full length FACS course online. My point is to tell you how all of this became such an important part of understanding people.

One of the things that Dr. Ekman has told me personally and has written about is the crux of this chapter—the one thing I hope you can take away: Just because you see someone's emotion doesn't mean you understand *why* the person is feeling that emotion—or displaying a facial microexpression, or *micro*, that is inconsistent with what is being said.

Once you learn to recognize and identify micros, you can change your communication style based on what emotion you see displayed, and then interject questions and elicitation to confirm the emotion you think you see. By using questions, conversation, and elicitation you will be able to pinpoint the true reasons for the emotion you saw. Dr. Ekman is developing an informative training tool, Responding Effectively to Emotional Expressions, or RE3, to help develop this skill set.

One word of caution: Be sure not to inject your own emotions into what you see or make assumptions about why someone is feeling a certain way. (Doing so would make you susceptible to the "Me Theory" error.) When you start a dialog, you can then determine why the emotion exists. Being able to understand the emotion helps you adapt and influence your target more.

Remember also that your goal as a social engineer is to become part of your targets' tribe. Doing so is easier when you give them more reason to feel you are just like them. For example, suppose you approach a group of strangers who are laughing and having a great time. You hang your head, your eyelids droop, and your lips are turned down—classic signs of sadness. Will the group want to get involved with you and your problems, or will they ignore you? If your goal is to get into that tribe, you can probably imagine that doing so will be harder if you look sad.

On the other hand, suppose your target is the sad person. Would you win him over by approaching him with a back slap, a loud laugh, and a few jokes? Or would you lower your voice, lower your body posture, and approach him softly, asking what's wrong?

Dr. Ekman and Dr. O'Sullivan started a program they named Truth Wizards. They identified a very small group of people who seemed to have a significantly above average ability to detect deception. My "scientific editor" for this book is Paul Kelly, also often referred to as PK in order to distinguish him from Dr. Paul Ekman; he has been identified as one of these Truth Wizards.

PK met Dr. Ekman after hearing a presentation about micros and learning that they were both involuntary and cross-cultural/universal. A very interesting facet of PK's communication skills is having been identified as a Truth Wizard from Dr. Ekman's and Dr. O'Sullivan's research on assessing credibility and detecting deception. These Wizards, approximately 50 in number, constitute the top one-third of one percent (99.666 percentile) of more than 15,000 people surveyed and have demonstrated a significantly higher accuracy rate (80 percent threshold) than average (53 percent). PK and I worked closely while I wrote this book to ensure that my work was solidly grounded in the science. In addition, when we ran into a few questions, we posed them to Dr. Ekman, who helped us stay on the path.

In my many conversations with PK, he talked about the power of being able to read these expressions, yet he gave the same caution as Dr. Ekman—just because you can see the expression doesn't mean you understand the reason for the emotion right away. As PK notes, micros *do not* answer the "why?" question, but they can often steer you toward finding that out. Dr. Ekman continued to identify people like PK from all walks of life and continued his research into these base emotions and the expressions attached to them.

To further help us with this task, Dr. Ekman broke what we are looking for into seven basic and culturally universal emotions, each with its own expressions and involuntary short-term muscular movements. They are fear, surprise, sadness, contempt, disgust, anger, and happiness. This chapter discusses each emotion in detail and offers many examples of what to look for. In addition, you will read stories and accounts from a veteran truth wizard that will help solidify these points and show you how any social engineer can learn to use these skills.

What Is a Truth Wizard?

In their Truth Wizards program, Dr. O'Sullivan and Dr. Ekman tested over 15,000 people and found that only 50 had a significantly above average ability to detect deception. This ability often included being able to read, detect, and decipher facial expressions. (Later, Dr. Ekman proved that learning to recognize and identify micros is a readily learnable skill.) This small number gave them only a few people to work with as a research pool. Regrettably, Dr. O'Sullivan passed away before she could publish her work about the Truth Wizards. In one interview, she described them as being "like Olympic athletes." O'Sullivan remarked, "Our wizards are extraordinarily attuned to detecting the nuances of facial expressions, body language and ways of talking and thinking. Although they seem to have a natural talent, they practice and are always paying careful attention. They tend to be older, too, with a lot of relevant life experience" (www.eurekalert.org/pub_releases/2004-10/ama-lad100804.php) Dr. Ekman noted, "We're still trying to find out how in the world did they learn this skill? Are they the Mozarts of lie detection; they just had it?" (www.onthemedia.org/story/131287-the-face-never-lies/transcript/).

Paul Kelly is among this group. As a former Secret Service agent, course director, and senior instructor at the U.S. Secret Service Academy, and adjunct faculty member at the NSA's National Cryptologic School, he has significant experience in dealing with all sorts of people. I have had the pleasure of meeting and working with PK and interviewing him for this portion of the book.

In our discussion, I wanted to first determine the difference between a macroexpression and a microexpression. PK helped me see that besides the duration (a microexpression is very fast, from 1/5 to 1/25th of a second; a macroexpression can last between 2 and 4 seconds), the main difference between the two is that macroexpressions are the emotional expressions people want you to see. On the other hand, a microexpression is involuntary, uncontrollable, and often telling of the true emotional content the individual is experiencing at that moment.

Of course, this made me ask him, if we can see microexpressions, does that automatically mean the target is being deceptive? PK told me that is a common misconception. A microexpression is a conscious suppression, or an unconscious repression of emotion displayed through these tiny expressions. Dr. Ekman uses the term *hot spot* to refer to a micro or any other display, verbal or nonverbal, that is inconsistent with what is being said or done. While not indicators of deception in and of themselves, an effective interviewer can use hot spots as inroads to finding the answer to the "why" question.

The question that inevitably arises is whether a talent for reading people can be used to tell if someone is lying. PK was adamant that there is no such thing as the "Pinocchio" clue. In other words, no single clue, even micros, tells you, in and of itself, that someone is lying. Figuring this out involves setting a baseline and looking for changes—hot spots—in the target's behavior, knowing how to ask questions, and following up by reading more expressions.

Just because a truth wizard has an above average ability to read people doesn't mean the rest of us can't learn. I am proof of that. I do not believe I fall into the same category as PK, but I have been studying under Dr. Ekman and his group for over two and a half years, and feel I have a pretty good handle on this skill now.

In working with PK he offered me these comments and tips:

1. If you see a hot spot, and begin to seek the answer to that important "why" question, do not focus on just one possibility. Instead, force yourself to develop an "alternate hypothesis" as to why the hot spot was displayed. Doing so will help to keep your objectivity.

2. Be an active listener and observer. Don't focus on one thing; utilize all five channels: face, body language, voice, voice style, and voice content.

3. Do not make a rush to judgment. Take all the time available before making a decision. Let the interview run its course. Let the speaker tell his or her story. Use all available verbal and nonverbal cues.

4. Note hot spots as they occur, but be selective as to when in the interview you follow up and/or challenge/confront the speaker.

One final piece of advice before I go on: All you know for sure is what you see, so don't make assumptions about why someone is displaying a certain emotion. Questions, baselines, and interview tactics are needed to truly delve into the why. This leads nicely into determining the difference between an emotion and a feeling.

Emotions versus Feelings

The seven base emotions I mentioned earlier are the basis of feelings. In *Emotions Revealed*, Dr. Ekman defines emotions as "a process, a particular kind of automatic appraisal influenced by. . .our personal past, in which we sense that something important to our welfare is occurring, and a set of psychological changes and emotional behaviors begins to deal with the situation" (13). To paraphrase, we can define emotions as the set of psychological rules that our mind has made up based on our previous history and biology to deal with whatever circumstance we are in currently.

We all have built-in instruction sets based on our childhood, mental makeup, and moral and personal belief structure. Imagine you are in the grocery store, and you overhear a mom scolding her child. She is doing so in a derogatory way, even calling the child stupid. What happens to you? Your brain automatically runs your "code" to determine how you feel. If your parents treated you that way, maybe you feel empathy and sadness for the child. Or maybe your parents were respectful and loving, so when you hear this, it triggers anger at the thought that a parent would act this way. The first few seconds after your brain starts to react, you probably cannot stop the program that will run. Code has been injected into your system, and muscular, psychological, and physical responses are triggered. The emotional trigger brings up feelings: resentment, annoyance, frustration, unhappiness. These feelings are the aftereffect of the emotion and the emotional trigger.

By understanding the resulting feelings, we also come to understand that emotions occur in degrees. For example, is love an emotion or a feeling? If you believe it's a feeling, you're right. Love often is called an emotion, but it is not one of the seven base emotions. Rather, it results from emotions and therefore is a feeling.

When we are happy, that can cause us to love. A surprise can cause us to love. Love also can be sad and can cause fear. Love itself is not "a set of psychological changes and emotional behaviors that begins to deal with" a situation. This distinction is important to remember.

The following sections dissect each emotion to help you understand how you can use them during communications.

Fear

Imagine you are watching a movie, and the music gets ominous as a woman walks through a dark room. The music tells you that something is about to happen; it has preloaded some emotional content for you. Suddenly, an assailant jumps out of a dark corner, wielding a knife. What happens?

You may gasp or scream. Your head and/or body might move back, away from the thing that is causing you fear. These things happen in response to the psychological decision that is "fight or flight." Your body is preparing for either—in this case, most likely it is flight!

Maybe even more telling is what occurs on your face when you are afraid. As shown in Figure 5-2, your eyebrows rise, your eyes widen, your mouth opens as you gasp, your lips pull back, and your face and body get tense.

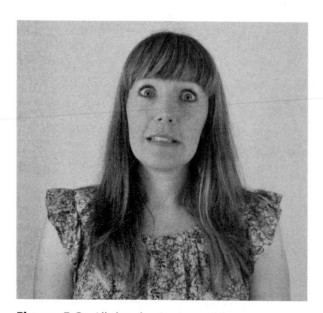

Figure 5-2: All the classic signs of fear

Note the tightness of the raised upper eyelids that show the white of the eye above the iris, and the horizontal pulling of the lips. If you saw this facial expression on a target, you probably could identify the emotional content within. However, someone who is afraid doesn't always display all of the physical responses just mentioned. Sometimes the signs of fear are much more subtle. Maybe the fear emotion doesn't actually scare you but instead worries you—an emotion closely linked with fear.

As I mentioned in the preceding section, feelings can define this emotion in more depth—feelings such as scared, afraid, petrified, terrified, worried, and panicked.

Suppose you are trying to gain access to a building while working as a professional social engineer. Your request needs to be approved, and the person you are talking to is worried about making the wrong decision but is trying to conceal his feelings. After you make your request, you might see the expression shown in Figure 5-3.

Figure 5-3: Signs of worry

When someone is worried, his eyebrows rise, and you see some tension in his forehead. In Figure 5-3, Ben is showing signs of worry that can confuse his fear with sadness. While the eyes, upper lids, brows, and mouth differ, a common feature is the isolated wrinkling of the central area of the forehead. His eyes may widen as he contemplates his decision. Since you now know that worry can be related to fear, an emotion that doesn't help us in this situation, how would you adjust your communication style to redirect the emotional content, or the script being run in the target's mind?

Because the script of fear/worry is already injected, stopping it may be hard. Therefore, you must alter or add to the frame to redirect the target's fear. For example, you may surmise that your request created worry in your target: "Should I let him in? What's the right decision?" Redirect the target's fear by saying something like "I understand this is an odd request, but management asked me to rush down here because of a situation. I don't like it any more than you do, but I need this job."

A statement like this may redirect the target's fear to his job, to upsetting management. This relieves him of responsibility and helps him make his decision.

Research has helped us understand that if we show fear/worry/panic on our faces, we only add to other people's emotions and raise more psychological red flags.

In these situations it is best to display a happy but not overly happy expression—a slight smile and head tilt indicating that you can be trusted.

The key point here is that you picked up on the emotional trigger— you saw a flash of worry or panic—and you must react to that emotion. Even though you are not completely sure why the person is feeling that emotion, you need to ensure that you can redirect it to another reason or emotion.

The Breakdown

Let me break down fear into each major part. This will help you notice this expression more clearly, reproduce it to influence others, and notice if you have a habit of showing this expression.

Here are some tips from PK and I to help you understand the movements involved in fear:

- Raise your upper eyelids as high as you can. If possible, tense your lower eyelids at the same time. With fear, one of the key distinctions is the wideness of the eyes, as shown in Figure 5-4.

- Pull your lips horizontally, as shown in Figure 5-5. Try saying the word "Eeek!" like you just saw a mouse—that expression draws the muscles of the mouth laterally
- Raise your eyebrows while tensing your upper eyelids to reveal the white of the eye above the iris.

Figure 5-4: The upper eyelids are raised, and the eyebrows are raised and pulled in.

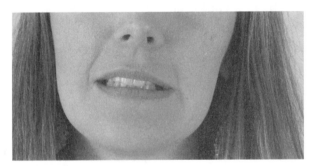

Figure 5-5: The mouth is laterally open, and the lips are stretched horizontally.

The fact that Selena's forehead and eyebrows are covered by her hair brings up an important point: Even with the face partially covered, we can clearly see that this is fear when we see both the eyes and mouth.

Practice these aspects of fear in a mirror, and notice any physiological changes that occur. If you have a hard time reproducing fear, stand in front of a mirror, open your eyes wide, and say "Eeeeeek!" while pushing your head back. That will create the mouth shape of fear and the neck tension that will help you see how this looks and know how it feels.

Surprise

Closely linked to fear, surprise has some similar displays. Fear and surprise are often confused. Suppose you have been traveling for a week on business. On the way back you have a nagging feeling that you have forgotten something important. You figure that you'll remember later, so you go home to rest.

You pull into your driveway. Your house is dark. You unlock and walk through the door and flip on the lights. Thirty people jump out and yell "Surprise!"

What happens? With surprise, the eyes open wide, the eyebrows rise, and the mouth drops open with an audible gasp (see Figure 5-6). Often the emotion of surprise causes the person to lean away at first, and then toward the object of surprise when he realizes he is safe.

Figure 5-6: The differences are subtle, but this is surprise, not fear.

What happens with this emotion? The body prepares for fight or flight, but in a situation like a surprise party, the other senses quickly see a nonthreatening scenario. The body leans toward the object of surprise. This can be followed by laughter and a smile. Dr. Ekman calls surprise a "gateway emotion" because it can lead to a number of other emotions, such as anger, happiness, and sadness when the result, or consequence, of the initial surprise is realized.

The implications for a social engineer are important. Surprise can be a gateway to a nice feeling after fight or flight determines you are not in danger. It is often followed by laughter, smiling, and some happiness. Therefore, this emotion can give you the upper hand when you're trying to influence someone.

Of course, I'm not suggesting that you hide in a closet and then jump out and yell "Surprise!" at your next social engineering penetration test. Let me illustrate the concept in another way.

In one engagement, I entered the building and walked up to the front desk to try to gain access. As I neared the counter, I noticed that the receptionist looked sad. Instead of going with my usual approach, I asked her, "Are you okay?" She told me she had lost one of her earrings. She was very upset because they were a gift from her husband and were expensive. I told her I was sorry and started to help her look for it. In a stroke of luck, I saw a glimmer in her hair; it was the earring. As she reached up and felt her hair, her facial expression was just like the one shown in Figure 5-6.

The receptionist was so happy that she never asked me who I was. After thanking me profusely, she just said, "Where were we?" I replied, "Oh, I was supposed to meet with HR. I just need a badge so that I can head over there for my meeting in five minutes." She handed me a badge and showed me the door in. In this case, surprise and the happiness that followed led to my success. Looking for ways to surprise your targets that don't entail jumping out of a closet can lead you to a successful ending.

The Breakdown

Taking the time to practice the steps in the breakdown will help you to gain experience in making, feeling, and seeing the expression more clearly.

The muscular movements involved in surprise are as follows:

- Raise your eyebrows while widening your eyes as much as possible, as shown in Figure 5-7. In surprise, however, the eyebrows are more arched/curved than in fear.
- Your jaw may unhinge slightly to open fully, as shown in Figure 5-8. (Think of the term "It was a jaw dropping experience!" or "When I told him, his jaw almost hit the floor!")
- You may audibly gasp while making an "Oh" sound.

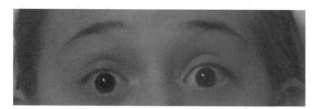

Figure 5-7: The eyes are wide, but even more so in fear.

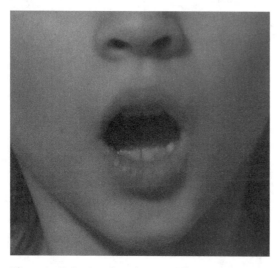

Figure 5-8: Notice the mouth opening: The lips are not pulled back.

Eyes displaying surprise are more relaxed, whereas eyes displaying fear are more tense and show more of the white. The eyebrows are more arched/raised in surprise.

In fear the teeth may clench or the mouth may drop open, but either way the lips are pulled back. Yet here in surprise we see that the lips are not pulled laterally toward the ears. Although it is not as pronounced in this picture, a classic expression of surprise would be shown with more of an "Oh" expression in the mouth, and the jaw would drop down more.

Surprise can be hard to distinguish from fear at first. But with practice, it can help you to understand the person's frame of mind.

Sadness

Some of my family is from Thailand, so I keep up with news from that part of the world. I was reading a story about a refugee camp in northern Thailand that caught on fire. A 15-year-old girl lost both her parents and a sibling in the fire. Not only was she in a refugee camp, but she was now all alone in the world. In a picture accompanying the story, her expression was one of extreme sadness.

As I read about this, I felt a sense of grief and emptiness, all for a person I have never met. Sadness can do that to us. Our human tribe mentality is so closely linked to empathy and compassion that these emotions come naturally to us and can easily influence our emotional content.

Sadness can range from mild discomfort to agonizing grief. Learning to read this emotion will help you communicate better and understand other people's emotional content. Learning to control slight displays of this emotion also can go a long way toward creating a feeling of empathy (closely linked to sadness) in the people you approach as a social engineer.

I once was hired to try to gain access to a building electronically. My goal was to load some malicious software onto the company's computer network using a USB key. The company wanted me to test its corporate policy that forbade employees from inserting foreign devices into any company machine.

I put on a shirt and tie, grabbed a manila folder, and filled it with a few "resumes" I had printed. My partner and I loaded a USB key with a resume that was also encoded with a piece of malicious code that would give us remote access to their network if clicked, or what is known as a "shell." I also had a good resume on there so when that one "failed," the target would have a good one to click.

I pulled up in the parking lot, opened my car door, and dumped a cup of coffee all over my folder of resumes.

As I entered the building, I knew I had to display true and appropriate levels of sadness for my ploy to work. I needed to show neither agonizing grief nor mild irritation. My expression was similar to the one Amaya is showing in Figure 5-9. As I walked up to the front desk with my dripping folder, the secretary greeted me with, "Oh, no, honey. What happened?" I quickly scanned her desk pictures and saw one of a small child with a cat.

"I've been out of work for a while, and I finally got an interview here today. I was driving here all nervous, and a cat ran out in front of me. I love cats, and I didn't want to hit it, so I swerved, and my coffee fell out of its holder onto my seat and drenched my resumes. Fortunately, I missed the cat, but I killed my resumes."

"Oh, that's terrible. What can I do to help?"

"I have my resume on this USB key. Could you print me just one copy, please?" I showed true sadness on my face as I handed her the USB key.

Moments later I had one resume printed, and I had received a text message saying "Shell" from my partner. The secretary then said, "What's your name? I can tell Ms. Jones you're here."

"Paul Williams. I have an 11 o'clock appointment with XYZ."

"Oh, sweetie, you *are* having a bad day. This is ABC. XYZ is next door."

"I'm so embarrassed! You've been so helpful, a lifesaver. I need to run so I won't be late. Thank you."

Figure 5-9: True sadness is complex but also creates an emotional bond.

I was out the door with a smile, a good feeling, a clean resume, and a remote connection to the company's network.

Was my facial expression the only reason I succeeded? No, not at all, but my expression added weight and believability to my story. If done right, this expression can make the person viewing it feel sadness, empathy, and compassion.

The caveat with this facial expression is that sometimes when we feel nervous, we can show sadness or fear. If your pretext is that you are confident, self-assured, and ready for action, but you show sadness, this can send mixed messages. Be cautious about leakage on your facial expressions.

The Breakdown

Sadness is a complex facial expression with many components. Understanding how to read, re-create, and display this facial expression is a powerful ability for any social engineer.

Sadness is composed of the following:

- The mouth may drop open, or remain closed but the corners of the lips are pulled down, as shown in Figure 5-10.
- Hold your lips in that position while raising your cheeks, similar to squinting.
- Look down while letting your upper eyelids droop, as shown in Figure 5-11.
- Another aspect in these photos is that the head may drop and the forehead may be tense, creating some isolated wrinkles there, as in Figure 5-11.
- Also, note that in classic expressions of sadness, the inner corners of the eyebrows come up and together, forming an inverted "V" shape (see Figure 5-11). Dr. Ekman notes that few people can direct this combination of AU movements intentionally. PK notes that those who can are likely to influence others favorably in evoking sympathy. He cites the actors Woody Allen and Nathan Lane as masters of their eyebrows, and now Amaya.

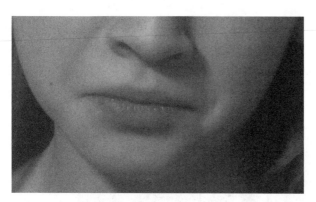

Figure 5-10: Even slightly downturned lips and raised cheeks create a clear picture of sadness.

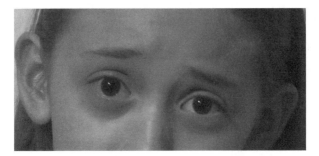

Figure 5-11: If the rest of the face shows nothing, sadness is still in the eyes.

In extreme grief we can see the mouth opened more and the lips turned down. In Figure 5-10, the sadness is subtle, yet you can see the corners of Amaya's mouth turning down.

One important point to remember is that sadness can be seen clearly in the eyes. Even if the mouth is not downturned, or the face is partially covered by clothing, we can see the emotion in the eyes.

One very hard aspect of sadness to control is the eyebrows, as shown in Figure 5-12. In some cases of sadness you see the following:

- The inner corners of the eyebrows go up, not the entire eyebrow.
- The brows are pulled up and together in the middle.
- The eyes still droop.
- A pouting protrusion of the center area of the lower lip

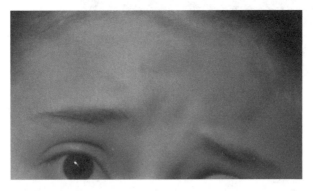

Figure 5-12: Eyebrow tension can indicate sadness.

The eyebrows alone can create a connection of sadness or empathy. This is a difficult skill to master. Dr. Ekman has stated that not many people can do it without feeling real sadness. Practice can make perfect (and an empathic link).

Contempt

In *Emotions Revealed*, Dr. Ekman says that "Contempt is only experienced about people or the actions of people but not about tastes, smells or touches."

Yixue Zhou, a researcher from the University of Pennsylvania, in the paper "Contempt and Self-Esteem," defines contempt as "an emotional reaction to a target individual or group who is perceived to be either morally or socially inferior to oneself."

Fischer and Roseman, in their research paper entitled "Beat Them or Ban Them: The Characteristics and Social Functions of Anger and Contempt," defined contempt further by saying that the purpose of contempt is to reject the object of the contempt from our social group or class.

From these various definitions, it's easy to see that contempt is a negative emotion that in a social engineering engagement we want to avoid displaying and definitely hope we never see in those we interact with.

In one interaction I had with a group of salespeople, I overheard a guy named Jim telling a group how many sales he had made that month. He didn't just point out his success, though. He also made sure that everyone knew he beat Ralph by mentioning Ralph's low sales numbers for the month. As the others walked away, I saw Ralph's face flash the emotion shown in Figure 5-13.

Figure 5-13: The unilateral display of contempt

Ralph quickly caught himself, smiled, and caught up with the group. He didn't want to be ousted from the tribe. I walked up to him and said, "Ralph, I'm new to the company, but listen, what that guy did was really stupid. He seems like an arrogant jerk."

Ralph looked at me as if I could read minds and said, "He isn't that bad. He just thinks more of himself…" and his voice trailed off.

"Well, either way, I'm sure you'll kick his butt next month."

By then we had approached the front door, which he held open for me as I tailgated into the company. He thanked me for the ego boost. He went his way, and I went mine. Being able to quickly read and react to facial expressions helped me see an opportunity to interact with someone on an emotional level that made him feel accepted. That interaction led me to success, and I was able to infiltrate the building.

Contempt is one of those emotions that I do not recommend mirroring. As a social engineer, I may see contempt and use it (as in the case of Ralph), but I do not want to add to that feeling. Contempt, if harbored, can turn into anger. Because it can lead you down a negative path, I like to leave this emotion behind.

The Breakdown

Contempt can include feelings such as superiority, smugness, or arrogance, and it is always unilaterally shown, or shown just on one side of the face, with one corner of the mouth pulled up, and the cheek and/or dimple on that same side accentuated. A social engineer needs to be able to pick out the signs and even subtle hints that a person may be feeling contempt. Look for these signs:

- One side of the face is raised, as if the cheek is pushing up to squint, as shown in Figure 5-14.
- The chin can be raised, as shown in Figure 5-13, making it easier to look down at the object of contempt.
- In many cases, contempt displays a raised cheek muscle on the same side of the face as the upturned asymmetrical lip, as shown in Figure 5-15.
- One you learn to recognize contempt, it is perhaps the easiest emotion (after happiness) to observe. You may be surprised at how often you see it, but remember the "why" question!

Figure 5-14: Notice the raised cheek.

When one side of the mouth and cheek is raised for contempt, it sometimes creates a sort of smirk. This unilateral display can be followed by a nod or another gesture indicating the feelings of arrogance.

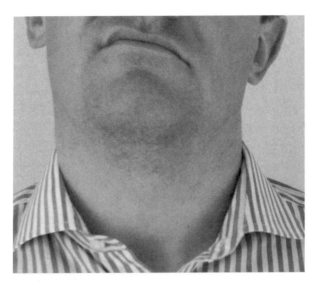

Figure 5-15: In this contempt expression, notice the asymmetrical turning of the lips.

I can't say this enough: Contempt is an easy emotion to miss for the untrained, but it's an important one to pick up. Once you learn to recognize contempt, it will jump out at you.

To illustrate the point about contempt, I'll relay a story PK told me of when he was able to see and use this expression. Once, while he was in an Arab country, his host invited PK to dine with him, but pointedly asked that they not order alcohol while at his table. This is a very common request in Islamic cultures. However, PK told me he noticed a micro of contempt appear on the face of one of his colleagues. Later, after developing rapport with the assistant he was told that the host was a "hypocrite" because he himself often imbibed alcohol while traveling abroad. The assistant, though junior to the host, likely felt he was the more devout Muslim because he never drank alcohol.

If you see it during an interaction and you are unsure why, reevaluate and assess quickly if you need to change something about your approach or body language. Ensure you are not being too aggressive in your approach or speech, and that you do not use any offensive language or jokes. In addition, before you even go out on an engagement make sure your appearance is not offensive in any way for the crowd you are targeting.

Disgust

While contempt is always directed toward a person, disgust can be triggered by a smell, taste, touch, sight, or even thoughts of something or someone—even yourself or your own actions. Disgust can trigger a strong physiological response in someone. When things disgust you, how do you feel? Some people gag at the sight of blood. Others feel sick when they think about vomit. Maybe while reading this short paragraph you started to display the expression shown in Figure 5-16.

Figure 5-16: In this disgust expression, we can see both disgust and hints of anger.

In my discussions with PK, he told me that disgust is often missed when people are tested on it and in real life because they don't recognize it for what it is. Yet training ourselves to see disgust when interacting with others can change our communications profoundly. When asked to name Ekman's seven universal emotions, most people list happy, sad, surprise, fear, and anger quite quickly. They seldom mention disgust or contempt, yet both are important to the social engineer. Though disgust is often confused with anger, each has its own unique characteristics.

Imagine a law enforcement officer interviewing a suspect, asking about a missing person, and seeing a flash of disgust on the suspect's face. What would that tell you? The officer needs to head down this avenue of questioning more deeply. The officer needs to find out if the suspect is disgusted at the officer or is imagining a scene of violence or something else that can bring up that emotion.

Once you are trained to see this expression, as PK puts it, "You will see it a lot more than you want to."

The Breakdown

Disgust is broken into a few different areas that the social engineer can try to pick up and use in interactions. Try to notice these signs:

- The nose wrinkles, as shown in Figure 5-17, almost as if to shut off the nose to an offensive smell. Often, wrinkles will appear on the bridge of the nose.
- The lips become furled and in some cases can even open, showing part of the teeth. Figure 5-18 shows disgust with both closed and open lips. In classic disgust, the upper lip is drawn up to the nose, exposing the upper teeth.
- The brow can become furrowed to an extent that the offensiveness of the object of disgust can cause irritation, as shown in Figure 5-19.

Figure 5-17: Notice the nose wrinkling.

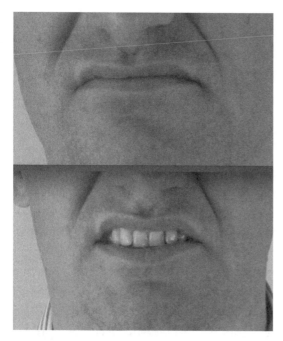

Figure 5-18: With disgust, the lips may be closed or open. Either way, you can see the lips furl, exposing the upper teeth almost in a snarl. The cheeks often sharply crease to form a large inverted "U" shape going from one cheek across the bridge of the nose, to the other.

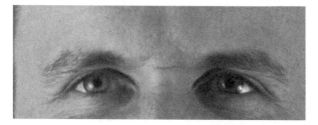

Figure 5-19: Disgust can be followed by anger or irritation, as shown in the eyes and eyebrows. Though the eyebrows may come somewhat down and together, as in anger, no glare of the eye is evident as in anger.

It is hard to breathe through the nose when this expression is in play. The body tries to block this offensive object from our smell and sight.

Disgust, obviously, is an unpleasant emotion. Even viewing someone who is showing it (as in Figures 5-17 through 5-19) can make you feel uneasy and irritable. As a social engineer, learning to see this expression can help you understand your target's emotional state and adapt your style.

Anger

Anger is an intense emotion that causes physical muscular tightness, In addition, increased heart rate, breathing, and feelings of irritation all follow. In *Emotions Revealed*, Dr. Ekman states, "One of the most dangerous features of anger is that anger calls for anger, and the cycle can rapidly escalate" (111). Later on in that same chapter he defines anger as one of the most dangerous emotions because it can cause someone to hurt the target of their anger.

When we are angry we lose our ability to think clearly and our reactions are ruled by this negative emotion. Chapter 8 discusses how strong emotions like anger can shut down our logic centers.

In one engagement, I pulled into the target company's parking lot and parked far from the front door. As I walked closer, I saw a man get out of his car parked in the VP parking spot. He was talking into his Bluetooth headset. I was too far away to hear the conversation, but what I saw was very close to what is shown in Figure 5-20.

Figure 5-20: All the classic signs of anger

I could tell this man was angry. As I got closer, I pulled out my phone to pretend I was answering, and then I slowed my pace so that I could hear what he was saying.

I overheard what sounded like a minor argument between the man and a vendor. This was a good opportunity for me to make a pretext change. From the comments he was making, I knew that the vendor he was talking to manufactured time clock systems. I walked in the door and up to the front desk and said, "Hi, I'm Paul. I'm here to check out your time card system. The boss told me you're having some major issues with your present vendor, and you wanted a competitive quote. Can you tell me where I can check the server?"

The receptionist took me through the locked doors to the server room and yelled to one of the IT guys: "Roy, Paul here needs to get in and check the time card system. He'll fix all our problems."

This is an instance in which seeing anger led to my success. Another example where I didn't do so well was one time when I was interact-ing with a target and he started talking about a female coworker in a derogatory way. I felt myself getting a little heated, and he must have seen something similar to what is shown in Figure 5-20, because he ended the conversation and walked away. As hard as it is, sometimes the social engineer needs to remove personal feelings and prejudices from the situation and allow the target the freedom of his or her opinions, no matter how contradictory they are to your own.

I once had a chance to interview a law enforcement interrogator. He told me about a case in which he arrested a suspect who was accused of peeping into women's bedroom windows and then pleasuring himself. He had a cowboy boot fetish, so if the woman had boots, that turned him on.

A few officers tried to get him to confess. We can almost picture the scene—an officer slamming his fist on the table or making threats. But all this anger in the room did not make the suspect open up. Then my friend went in and sat down calmly, no anger or disgust on his face. He said, "You know, I love when a woman wears cowboy boots too. My favorites are the natural brown ones."

After looking at the officer for a few moments he exclaimed, "Brown?, You haven't seen anything till you've seen *red* boots."

From then on the conversation was open, and the suspect confessed to all his transgressions. A social engineer has to work hard to remove traces of anger from his facial expressions, or this can lead to judgmental feelings and a disastrous outcome for his engagements.

The Breakdown

A lot of things happen during the emotion of anger. Just think about what happens when you feel angry. Do you breathe heavier? Do you get tense? All of this is normal. The body is preparing for a fight, so the muscles tense up, breathing may get heavier, the chin lowers to protect the neck, and the hands may clench.

In addition, the face displays a lot of tension and furrowing. Recreate these with caution, as you will feel angry:

- Pull your eyebrows down and together, almost like you're trying to touch your nose to the inner part of your eyebrows, as shown in Figure 5-21.
- While you are doing this, try to create a glare (shown in Figure 5-21.
- Your lips are pressed together tightly. Or, if they are open, as in Figure 5-22, your teeth are clenched, with a tight jaw.
- The chin often is lowered to protect your neck. (Fight not flight!)

Figure 5-21: The brow furrowing and stare are intense.

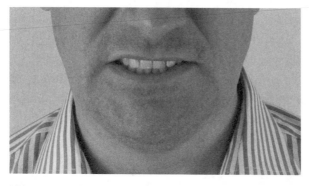

Figure 5-22: A tense jaw and clenched teeth are indicators of anger.

These pictures don't show intense anger, but these subtle hints are still important to notice. When you look at this expression, even with its subtle hints, as a whole it is much easier to pick up this anger emotion.

In Figures 5-21 and 5-22, Ben is showing classic but subtle signs of anger. The brow is not as furrowed as it may normally be when someone is intensely angry. Learn to recognize and, even more importantly, control this emotional display, and it can truly help you influence your targets.

Happiness

One thing I learned from Dr. Ekman that profoundly affected me was that microexpressions are muscular movements in reaction to neurological responses to emotional triggers. Yet the reverse is also true. If I make facial expressions on purpose, I can create a neurological response and emotion.

That is why I chose to end this chapter with the emotion of happiness. I hope that as you finish this chapter you will have a smile on your face.

A smile, linked to true happiness, is a powerful tool. Happiness is the most readily recognized emotion. Perhaps you're smiling now, just reading these words. Can you see yourself smiling when you look at a laughing baby? Don't you find it interesting how, when you hear other people laughing, it makes you laugh or at least feel happier?

Happiness triggers happiness in a powerful way. It is because of this that learning the difference between a real smile and a fake one is so important.

In 1862 a doctor named Guillaume-Benjamin-Amand Duchenne wrote *The Mechanism of Human Physiognomy*, which is about a series of tests he performed across France. He used portable electric machines to shock some muscles on people's faces. He could get them to show all sorts of expressions just by stimulating the muscles that controlled those emotions.

His research gave rise to the term "Duchenne smile." It is characterized by raising the corners of the mouth, controlled by the zygomatic major muscles, and raising the cheeks, which produces crow's feet at the eye corners, controlled by the orbicularis oculi. See the contrast between Figures 5-23 and 5-24.

Dr. Ekman often refers to the *sincere* smile versus the *polite* smile. In a sincere smile, shown in Figure 5-23, we can see that Selena's mouth and eyes are engaged. The wrinkles on the outer corners of the eyes, sometimes called "crows' feet," are a characteristic of the sincere smile. In fact, you can see happiness in her eyes even if you can't see her mouth. In addition, there is a "twinkle" in her eyes that just doesn't exist with the "social smile," shown in Figure 5-24.

Figure 5-23: With the Duchenne smile, the mouth is raised, and the eyes are involved.

Figure 5-24: The "social smile" does not involve the eyes.

If you display a social smile, the average person may not look at you and think, "Wow. That person is using only her zygomatic major and not the orbicularis oculi. That smile is definitely fake." But the person may feel uneasy because she senses that you are not displaying a true emotion.

A social engineer wants to make her target smile, feel good, and always view her as trustworthy. A sincere smile does all that. In their study "The Value of a Smile: Game Theory with a Human Face," researchers Scharlemann, Eckel, Kacelnik, and Wilson indicate that the simple act of smiling creates a bond with the person you are interacting with, telling him that you are trustworthy and want to encourage his happiness. To read the full article, visit www .sciencedirect.com/science/article/pii/S0167487001000599.

Knowing all this, it behooves the social engineer to ensure that he or she can master this emotion despite nervousness, fear, anger, and other feelings. What helps is mixing in other aspects, such as a head tilt (discussed in the next chapter), open ventral displays (discussed in Chapters 3 and 4), and a lower tone of voice (discussed in Chapter 2).

The Breakdown

Follow these steps to create a sincere smile:

1. Start by thinking about something that makes you happy.
2. Raise your cheeks while bringing up the corners of your lips, as shown in Figure 5-25.
3. Without squinting, raise your cheeks. Doing so pushes up your eyes, giving you crow's feet (see Figure 5-26).

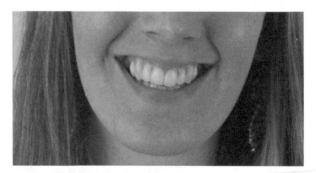

Figure 5-25: Notice the way the cheeks are raised bringing the lips up in a smile. The sincere smile involves much more of the face—the mouth, the cheeks, the chin—and some blushing may even occur.

Figure 5-26: The eyes are where we see the true happiness.

The more you look at the eyes of someone who is smiling sincerely, the happier you will be. This is because of how our brains take in emotion. The more we view an emotional display, the more easily we can feel this emotion.

After reading all the information in this chapter, you might be wondering how you can practice recognizing these emotions.

Perfect Practice Makes Perfect

Part of being a social engineer or protecting yourself from malicious social engineers is learning how to mimic and recognize the skills they use. Learning to read faces is not as hard as it sounds. Researchers such as Dr. Ekman have spent their lives studying this topic and developing tools to help people learn how to recognize the meanings behind facial expressions and body language. I have used training tools such as Dr. Ekman's Microexpression Training Tool (METT) and METT Advanced Tool to continually hone my skills. I also use them in my training classes to help my students learn.

These are not the only methods, though. My learning began with Dr. Ekman's *Emotions Revealed* and a mirror. I sat in front of that mirror and moved my face in the way described in each section of the book. I did this both looking in the mirror and not, trying to see if I could feel the difference in my face. I did this repeatedly until I thought my facial movements resembled what was shown in the book. After that, I began to analyze the emotions those movements brought up in me to make sure they matched.

From there I began to watch people close to me to see if I could notice macro facial expressions. From there I began trying to find one microexpression at a time. For example, after I finished practicing anger in the mirror, I knew about the angry stare, the brow furrowing, the tight lips and jaw, the chin being lowered. I began looking at my family and friends for subtle hints of these signs. I was amazed at what I saw. It was like a new world opened up. I could look at a family member and discern a true emotion during a conversation. Then I started making the classic rookie mistake: I believed that because I saw the emotion, I knew why the emotion was happening. Making that mistake led to a lot of frustration at first. Once I learned to reign in that impulse, I began to see the emotion and realize I needed to learn more about it. I improved my ability to communicate with my kids, wife, friends, and others.

Then I saw the business implications and began to realize that I could use my nonverbal communication skills to influence other people's emotions.

I found that the more I practiced, the quicker and more accurate I became. After one five-day class I taught, a student asked me if this ability can be shut off. It can't. Although I don't always have to react to or use the information I gather, once you know something, it's hard to turn it off.

I liken this to learning a foreign language. I traveled to China and Hong Kong a few times, and to make the trips easier, I started to study Chinese. After a few lessons I was amazed at how often I would hear the handful of words I knew when at a Chinese restaurant or the Asian market.

It's the same with facial expressions. The more you know, the more you will start to pick up and "hear" without trying. This is why there are really two rules about learning to read faces: The old adage is usually "practice makes perfect," but practicing the wrong way won't make you perfect. So let's change that to "perfect practice makes perfect," and secondly don't think you know the *why* behind someone's emotion.

Summary

The face reflects your emotional content both in conscious macros and involuntary micros. Learning to read that content—and recognizing "hot spots" (contradictions) can enhance your skill as a professional social engineer and your ability to catch a malicious person in action.

On a more personal level, learning about the face can help you learn more about yourself and how you interact with others. It will help you create long-lasting relationships, communicate better, and understand those around you more deeply.

In one class I was running in Dublin there was a very energetic young female student from Germany. She loved the psychology behind human interaction and had a natural talent for interaction. When I took them out on engagements I caught a picture of her "focus" face. It showed classic signs of anger.

I was able to work with her to show her what she was doing and it helped her in future communications. This self-awareness can really help to hone your skills and control your emotional content.

Sometimes when I am training people on facial expressions they feel overwhelmed. There are so many moving parts, and so many aspects to look for. When people say that, I start off with a lesson on something a little easier before we launch them into the more detailed work.

That lesson is the difference between signs of comfort and discomfort and that is the topic for the next chapter.

6

Understanding Nonverbal Displays of Comfort and Discomfort

Comfort zones are most often expanded through discomfort.

—Peter McWilliams

Whenever I teach a class about social engineering, I cover body language and facial expressions, in a similar manner to the previous chapters of this book. Some students are overwhelmed by all the things they are told to look for and feel that trying to notice too many things will distract them. Instead of trying to come up with tricks to help them notice all the expressions or signs, I tell them to do one thing: Look for signs of comfort and discomfort. Noticing that someone has a certain baseline body language that changes to discomfort can tell you a lot as a social engineer. PK, one of the "truth wizards" mentioned earlier, notes that Dr. Ekman refers to such changes in baseline as "hot spots." Dr. O'Sullivan, who coordinated research on the "wizard project," noted that the wizards often cited recognition of such displays while observing their subjects as a factor in their assessments.

Imagine that your target is Ben. Your goal is to start a conversation that will lead to elicitation. As you approach him, you see him sitting with his hands behind his head and a contented look on his face, as shown in Figure 6-1.

As you start speaking to him, your conversation starts to move toward a few questions about his company, and then he displays what is shown in Figure 6-2.

As Ben contemplates his decision, he starts feeling uncomfortable. His neck muscles tense, and he begins wondering if he is making the right decision by continuing the conversation and answering your questions. He goes from a confident pose to one of high discomfort.

Figure 6-1: Ben is content and feeling comfortable and confident.

Figure 6-2: What has changed with Ben?

For the social engineer, this is a huge tell. You can clearly see the emotion Ben is feeling and how it affects him. At this point, a smart social engineer will quickly determine if he can push harder or back off, depending on the goals of the engagement.

This short chapter is about noticing these subtle or not-so-subtle signs of comfort and discomfort and how a social engineer can use them. The following sections break this topic into a few areas you can watch for.

Neck and Face Pacifying

In addition to the neck-rubbing behavior just discussed, the social engineer can notice other signs that can be strong indicators of discomfort. The key is to watch for a change in behavior that indicates that something is making the target uncomfortable.

Similar to when a man rubs the back of his neck, when a woman feels scared, threatened, or worried, she often covers the area of her neck called the suprasternal notch, as shown in Figure 6-3.

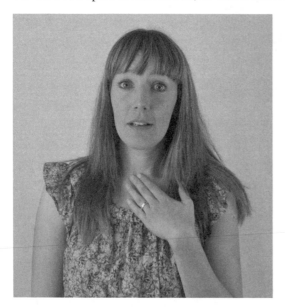

Figure 6-3: This neck-pacifying move shows discomfort.

I have spoken with people who have reviewed security videotapes after a child has gone missing in a store. They have noticed that the first thing the mother does is the gesture shown in Figure 6-3.

Another thing that a social engineer may see is a baseline of comfort transition into face rubbing, as shown in Figure 6-4.

These moves, when noticed, can tell the social engineer that the person is feeling threatened, unsafe, or uncomfortable with the decision or situation at hand. Dr. Ekman and other psychologists might classify such nonverbal movements as "manipulators."

Figure 6-4: Rubbing the face like this is pacifying.

When you're trying to make hard choices, it can be comforting to rub or touch two nerves that run through the neck and upper chest—the vagus nerves and the carotid sinus.

What to Watch For

As a social engineer, watch for changes in these behaviors. It is important to notice if someone is comfortable when you first approach him but then starts rubbing his face or neck. If you see this happen, quickly determine whether something about you or something you said caused this behavior.

I was talking to a law enforcement agent once about face and neck rubbing. He told me about a time when he went to a home to inquire about the whereabouts of a relative of the residents, who was fleeing from the law. Every time my friend brought up the person's name and a certain location on their property—the garage—he noticed that the mom would move her hand to her neck, as seen in Figure 6-3. After seeing this happen a couple of times, he decided to pose the question twice more. He then asked if police could search the premises since she had nothing to hide. After she said yes, he went straight to the garage and found the person he was looking for hiding there.

Watch for these changes in behavior to give you "tells" about someone's emotional content. Once you understand that something is causing a change, if the change is desirable, decide whether to throw in some elicitation questions that will confirm your suspicion.

In one engagement in which I had a chance to use these skills, I was tasked to get past third-party security guards into a large warehouse. The rule was that the security guard had to have the photocopy of any visitor's government-issued photo ID (driver's license or passport, for instance) before the visitor was allowed in.

Getting through the mantrap and to the security desk was not difficult, but then at the front desk the security guard said, "Before I issue you a badge please give me your driver's license for a photocopy."

I generally leave my wallet in the car when doing engagements, so I first used a discomfort sign: I raised my hand and rubbed the back of my neck, and while looking back at the very large metal mantrap I said, "Oh man, I'm sorry, I left it in the car in my wallet." I noticed a stern look on the security guard's face, and before he could speak his command to tell me to take the walk of shame, I said, "Wait, all you need is an official picture ID identifying me as the person I say I am?"

"Um, yeah, basically."

"Then will a company ID do?" I said, before continuing,

"Oh excellent, then I am OK." Then, relaxing my face and body, I pulled out my fake corporate ID: "This ID has my picture and the barcode here contains all my personal details. You can just photocopy this."

Moments later I was being handed a visitor's badge and escorted into the facility.

Another thing to remember as a social engineer is that these gestures give off the feeling that a person is uncomfortable. You can use this feeling to influence someone's emotional content. For example, if you are trying to pretext as someone who has shown up at a company late for and nervous about a job interview, displaying this action can add credibility to your pretext.

Mouth Covers

While reading a newspaper or magazine story about some disaster, it is not uncommon to see people at the scene displaying what is seen in Figure 6-5.

Figure 6-5: Mouth open and covered in shock or surprise

As mentioned in Chapter 5, when we are scared or surprised, we gasp to prepare for the "fight or flight" response. It is believed that we cover our mouths as an automated response to self-comfort, much as we self-comfort using face and neck touching. The shock, surprise, or fear is followed by a feeling of discomfort, which is followed by self-comforting actions.

If you see a calm baseline change to the type of action shown in Figure 6-5, reevaluate your approach and make sure you are not the one who is causing the shock.

What to Watch For

If you observe someone covering his or her mouth, try to figure out what could be causing this action. Remember the importance of the "why" question that Dr. Ekman stressed. Is the display followed by anger, sadness, or fear? These emotions should alter how you proceed. You can use them to become a member of a tribe if the reaction is to a public event.

Imagine being at the scene of a crime or witnessing some horrible event. While everyone else is mouth covering, gasping, and looking away, you see one person in the crowd with a big smile on his face. What would you think? He has not fit into the tribe; he stands out, and not in a good way. Similarly, as a social engineer, notice the crowd you are approaching and if they are shocked or surprised by an event; an easy way to start fitting into the tribe is to take on the emotional content of the crowd around you.

For example, on 9/11 I was standing near a group of strangers when the news showed the second plane hitting the second tower. The shock and horror that caused many gasps were followed by all of us becoming one tribe very fast. We bonded over the emotions from that event and our reactions.

As disturbing as it is to discuss looking for—or, even worse, creating—a situation in which you use a major event as a tool to join a tribe, unfortunately malicious attackers use this tactic all the time.

I do not recommend that a social engineer use this display without a good reason to. The person you are interacting with will be confused or even angry if he feels he was made to feel shock or fear for no reason.

Lips

The lips are a huge source of information on comfort versus discomfort. This is not just because they form words, but, maybe even more importantly, because of what they do when words are *not* being used.

Sometimes the lips tell us that the person wants to say something but is holding back. The lips also can tell us that someone is nervous or lacking in confidence. Learning to pick up on these subtle signs can give you that extra edge as a social engineer.

Suppose you're at work, and you're dealing with a manager you dislike. You say something a bit harsh to her, and she gives you a look like the one shown in Figure 6-6.

As she looks at you, her lips are pursed, as shown in Figure 6-6. Tight lips are a sign of anger, even when that anger is suppressed. In essence, pursed lips hold the mouth shut to keep you from forming the words you may desperately want to say. Pursed lips can also indicate that the person is deciding whether to take some action—deciding between possible actions or reactions.

Another sign to watch for is the puckered lip. Similar to a pursed lip, it can indicate that words are being held back, but there is no anger. Instead, this display indicates uncertainty. Suppose you ask someone a question she is unsure how to answer. Would you see a response similar to Figure 6-7?

Selena looks a little indecisive in this image. She was asked a question and is deciding how to answer.

In Figure 6-8, Ben shows a little more discomfort. Not only is he unsure whether he wants to answer, but he also is showing some signs of frustration with the questions being asked. His eyebrows coming down and together can reflect cognitive load (thinking)—and possibly anger. Look for signs of lip puckering after a difficult question is asked to see if the person you are talking to is showing signs of discomfort.

Figure 6-6: Pursed lips are tight like in anger.

Figure 6-7: Showing some signs of uncertainty

Figure 6-8: Discomfort and uncertainty

Although by itself none of these is a clear sign of deceit, if a social engineer sees these signs, he or she can target that area of information to see if deception is in play.

One last lip display I will discuss is one of high discomfort. Lip biting indicates anxiety, as shown in Figure 6-9.

Figure 6-9: Lip biting and signs of anxiety

As shown in Figure 6-9, you can see anxiety not only in Selena's lip display, but also in her eyes. The wideness of her eyes is similar to what you might see in fear or surprise, indicating she may be feeling anxious. Some people have a habit of doing this, so notice when it starts and stops, because it can indicate a baseline; then look for changes. Generally this display occurs when someone feels anxious.

Sometimes the lips are not the only things that get bitten when someone feels anxious. You may also see displays similar to Figures 6-10 and 6-11.

Figures 6-10 and 6-11 both show a display that can indicate contemplation, anxiety, or thought (cognitive load).

Figure 6-10: Finger biting is another sign of anxiety or nervousness.

What to Watch For

In all these lip displays, a social engineer would be smart to look for changes. Notice when a person starts these displays, and remember the conversation or questions that occurred at the time. Similarly, a person licking his/her lips, along with all the other lip displays, can fall into the category of nonverbal manipulators. An increase in displaying manipulators is a departure from a baseline—and can be a hot spot for you to note.

These can all be indicators of stress, anxiety, or holding back—all good signs that discomfort is setting in or has set in.

As a social engineer, you should notice if your communication is causing this reaction and then adjust your behavior. Similar to other areas mentioned in prior sections, you can use your own lip displays, subtly, to influence someone's emotions.

Figure 6-11: Object biting or chewing can indicate nervousness or contemplation.

For example, when you ask someone for a favor, a little lip bite or pucker can show that it is difficult for you to ask, eliciting sympathy from the person. Or suppose you're telling a story, and you get to the details of how you might lose your job if this task doesn't get done. Displaying some lip pursing can add weight to your story, showing how difficult it is for you to say what you have to say.

Whether you are watching for these signs or using them, learning to recognize their meanings can make a huge difference in your success as a social engineer.

Eye Blocking

Often when someone is extremely sad, she squeezes her eyes shut or even covers them, as shown in Figure 6-12. Why? A physiological response causes us to block or cover the object making us sad. This same display can be seen when someone is not extremely sad but is trying to block an object that irritates, saddens, or angers her.

Figure 6-12: Eye blocking is a classic sign of sadness.

If you see the person you are engaged with displaying this sign, it is a good idea to analyze the topic of conversation—the "why" question—and see if it is a basis for this emotion.

When I was young, a popular kind of insult began with "Your mom" or "Your mama." It seemed to fit any situation, and it generally brought smiles and laughter. One time I was with a close friend, and we were trading insults when I threw in a "Your mom." I was met with something similar to the image shown in Figure 6-12 and then some tears. I had forgotten that, only a couple weeks before, my friend's mom had died. My insensitive and callous remark caused her to think about her painful loss, and she tried to block out the object of that pain: me.

What to Watch For

If you see an eye-blocking display, and it was not caused by something you said, the best question to ask is, "Is everything okay?" There's no quicker way to build rapport with another person than to notice that she is in pain and to show concern.

As terrible as it sounds, this display can also be used to elicit sympathy from people. Showing this display subtly and at the right time can create a feeling of sorrow for you and cause someone to approach you and ask if you are all right. Con men and social engineers have used sympathy and assistance themes for years.

Self-Comforting and Head Tilts

I always find this portion interesting. In the 1980s, so-called "sales gurus" used to teach that if someone crossed his arms, this meant that he was uninterested and closed off. Research has helped us see that this is a wrong conclusion. Some people stand like that simply because it is comfortable, others because they are cold, and still others because of habit.

But a social engineer can look for something that can help determine a person's change in emotion from a baseline. Mainly women assume a stance that is considered self-comforting. They fold their arms across their bodies, under their breasts, as shown in Figure 6-13.

Figure 6-13: Self comforting and a sign that something may have changed

The key is to notice if the display starts at a particular point. Suppose you approach a group and notice a woman standing with her arms at her sides. She sees you coming and crosses her arms. This may be a good point at which to analyze your approach to see if it is causing her discomfort.

Reviewing the circumstances, the surroundings, and what might have changed can give you a good indication of emotional changes. A good social engineer will analyze a person's level of discomfort, try to determine the cause through observation and questions, and then adjust accordingly.

The last comfort display I will discuss in this chapter is head tilts. This concept is similar to open ventral displays. A good head tilt, combined with a smile, is a powerful tool. Just remember that the smile must be genuine, and the head tilt must be subtle. A fake smile and severe head tilt will make you look deranged, not trustworthy. But the proper angle will give you a powerful sense of trustworthiness and friendliness, as shown in Figure 6-14.

Figure 6-14: The comfort of a good head tilt and smile

Here Ben displays a genuine smile and a subtle head tilt. This display says, "I trust you, and I'm happy to see you, so you can trust me." This high-comfort display creates a warm feeling in the person you are interacting with, as shown in Figure 6-15. This display says to the person you are talking to, "I trust you, so you can trust me."

Selena is happy, trusting, and ready to participate in this relationship. You can see that her whole face is involved in the smile, and her head tilt, not as subtle as Ben's, says that she is open.

Mixing the head tilt and smile with an open ventral display is a powerful tactic. Former U.S. president Bill Clinton had this down pat. He would hold up his palms, smile, tilt his head, and invite you to join his cause. He won the hearts of the American people using this nonverbal display.

Figure 6-15: Selena's not-so-subtle head tilt says she is open to this relationship.

Former U.S. vice presidential candidate Sarah Palin also tried to use this display. She had a great smile and a good head tilt, but when she used her open ventral displays, she often added a shrug to the mix. This one gesture made her seem unsure of herself and her message.

What to Watch For

As a social engineer you want to watch yourself when it comes to this display. When you get nervous, you become tense, and tension will make you look rigid and stiff. If you're tense, you won't be able to give a good head tilt and smile. So, firstly, watch your own displays and make sure you are showing the proper emotions for your pretext.

Also, I know I said this a lot in this section, but I can't tell you how important it is to continually watch for subtle changes in the baseline that can be hot spots. Recently my wife was telling me about a situation in which she was with some friends. While telling the story, she had a warm smile, and she was open. I asked her about a particular person and she crossed her arms in front of her, her voice lowered and she became stiffer. At that point, I knew something had happened between them, but I also knew I couldn't just ask, "What happened?"

I said, "Hey, are you OK? You seem tense."

"Well…," she contemplated telling me or not, "actually I am. Let me tell you what happened." And I got the full story. Being alert to changes in the person you are talking to can give you enough to change your body language, then change your conversational style to elicit more information.

Summary

Herein lies a lesson for all those interacting with other people: Nonverbal displays influence how others view you, so use them wisely, use them with caution, and use them with practice. If you want people to feel comfortable and at ease, then you must practice conscious application of nonverbal displays.

Also note any negative or discomfort displays that can hurt your interactions. They can be useful to back up a pretext, but use caution.

Noting levels of comfort and discomfort is a good starting point for you to begin your journey into deciphering nonverbal communications. Learning to pick up, use, and control the displays you make can change how you communicate for the better. Even more powerful, it can change how others view you.

As you finish this chapter on nonverbal communication, some questions are left unanswered. Primarily, can these actions be controlled? Can you pinpoint the location in the brain that controls nonverbal language? The next chapter covers all of this and much more.

III Deciphering the Science

7

The Human Emotional Processor

Let's not forget that the little emotions are the great captains of our lives and we obey them without realizing it.

—Vincent Van Gogh

I t is an oversimplification to say that our brains are similar to computers. A computer has a series of hardware components that all interact to create the desired output.

As you double-click the mouse to open a program, code is run to call a request for memory in your computer to be allocated for the program. The kernel of the computer then will load the code for the program into memory, and then it jumps to a particular area of memory and starts running the program. If all goes as planned, you get a graphical output from your desired input. As I typed this sentence, I pressed keys on the keyboard that triggered code inside the computer to use both its memory and processing power to put the desired letters on the screen. If I just bang away on my keyboard, I will get gibberish. If I close my eyes and type without thought or without looking, I will get gibberish. Sure, there is a chance that some of it will spell words and make sense, but it is unplanned and unfocused.

This is not much different from our brains and emotional content and how we process it. Our senses take in external stimuli (much like using the keyboard and mouse). Our memory, or life experiences mixed with actual memories (what is in our storage), appraises how that content triggers emotions and responses. Our internal processors (like a computer processor) trigger code that runs and tells us how to respond based on previous experience and present "processing power" (i.e., how is your emotional content at this time?).

Understanding this is key to understanding nonverbal communication. Engaging with humans while ignoring this type of knowledge is equivalent to just "banging on the keyboard." You will have some success, maybe even a few good lines, but overall you will produce gibberish.

One important point to remember is that our emotion affects our perception and reaction to a situation. For example, when I was young I used to love eating eggs. My mom would make what she called "egg in the bread" (I know, not very ingenious). She cut out a circle in some white bread, fried it in a pan, and cracked an egg in the middle. I looked forward to the buttery goodness of this breakfast.

We kept chickens, so we always had fresh eggs. One day I ran out, grabbed a few eggs, and started to make my favorite breakfast. As I cracked the first egg into the pan, a bloody half-formed chick emerged. I gagged and started to heave. The sight of a tiny chick in a frying pan was so disturbing that I couldn't eat eggs again for almost 12 years. In this instance the emotions that were linked to that scene were so strong that it took me over a decade to control the disgust emotion linked to the thought of eggs. That emotion modulated my perception and affected my memories, triggering a very strong reaction.

Because each person's memories, life experiences, and emotions are different, we should not assume that our emotions or feelings on a matter are the same as the person we are interacting with.

Emotional responses to a situation can differ greatly from one person to the next. In addition, our "processors" will try to figure out how relevant the stimulus is before they give us the emotional reaction. In 1960 Dr. Magda Arnold published a work titled "Emotion and Personality" that stated that our emotional appraisal process is unintentional and automatic. Although some researchers disagree, most agree that emotion involves an appraisal process that occurs in our internal processors to create a response.

What is this processor? The easy answer is the brain. But the brain is so complex and carries out so many functions, can we really pinpoint an area that is responsible for this processing?

Introducing the Amygdala

In their 2002 paper titled "The human amygdala: a systematic review and meta-analysis of volumetric magnetic resonance imaging," researchers Brierley, Shaw, and David describe the amygdala (pronounced uh-*mig*-dull-uh) as "an almond shaped mass of gray matter located within the anteromedial, or the front toward the middle, part of the temporal cortex" (see Figure 7-1).

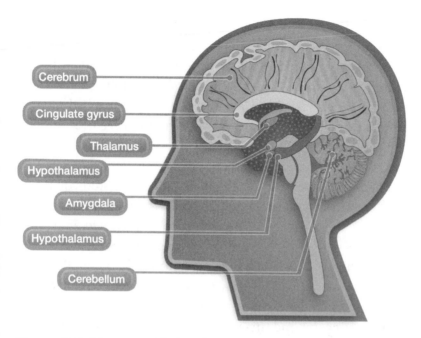

Cerebrum

Cingulate gyrus

Thalamus

Hypothalamus

Amygdala

Hypothalamus

Cerebellum

Figure 7-1: The amygdala is a tiny portion of the brain that processes emotion.

Additional research indicates that the amygdala has a dense core of nerve nuclei that processes input from all modalities, or senses. In essence, all our sensory input passes through this area of our brain and then is projected to various brain regions.

Researcher D.G. Amaral states in his 1992 research that "the amygdala has dense projections to many brain regions, including the brain stem, hypothalamus, hippocampus, basal ganglion and the cortical regions." These regions all play a part in processing emotions and our responses.

How the Amygdala Processes Information

Wataru Sato from Kyoto University in Japan released an excellent paper titled "The Information Processing Role of the Amygdala in Emotion." He breaks down the processing roles of the amygdala and how our sensory inputs and outputs are affected by that processing.

One of the studies referenced in his work talks about how emotion can be elicited from someone without his or her conscious awareness of the stimuli. To prove this, a study done by Kochiyama Sato in 2004 showed negative (angry) and neutral (no emotion) slides subliminally to the patient's unilateral visual fields. He found that the patients had a higher electrodermal response to the negative slides than to the neutral ones.

Combining this research with other work suggests that emotional processing by the amygdala can occur subconsciously and can be affected by sensory input. Combine that with the 2002 study by Dr. H. Oya titled "Electrophysiological responses in the human amygdala." Dr. Oya's research indicates that the amygdala is activated as soon as 50 to 150 milliseconds after the stimulus is presented. Since it has been proposed that the visual cortices activate at around 200 to 300 milliseconds, the rapid activity of the amygdala could point to the fact that it is processing this emotion subconsciously.

As a social engineer, I find this combination of research fascinating. I interpret it to mean that our brains (amygdalas) start processing the stimuli presented to them on a subconscious level before the individual even begins to thoughtfully process these cues. While embedded with U.S. combat troops in Afghanistan, author Sebastian Junger, in his book *War*, made several observations about the amygdala. It can process an auditory signal in 15 milliseconds, but, though fast, can only trigger a reflex and wait for the mind to catch up. He also noted that the amygdala requires only a single negative experience to decide that something is a threat. These stimuli include facial expressions, clothing, and other visual cues, as well as sounds, smells, and other sensory input.

This discussion demonstrates that good social engineers need a lot of information on their targets. Knowing what likes, dislikes, hobbies, problems, and so on are part of the target's life helps the social engineer avoid any looks, expressions, or clothing styles that may be negative or offensive to the target. Information also helps the social engineer see what topics should or should not be discussed.

If all this is true, there must be a way to hijack someone's amygdala to create emotional content that you want there—to influence the person to have emotions that will make your job easier.

Hijacking the Amygdala

Suppose you are sitting at your desk, frustrated. Your work is piling up, and there seems to be no end in sight. Due to budget cuts, some of your team has been let go. Your phone is ringing. You have three meetings scheduled for today. Your spouse texts you that the car needs to be fixed. Your email dings. Your coworker is telling you that the report you sent has incorrect data, and you need to fix it pronto and to avoid handing in such shoddy work. You click Reply and type a terse, angry email that sets him straight. Right after you click Send, a sense of relaxation comes over you, followed by dread. You go to your Sent folder, read what you just wrote, and begin to wonder if jumping out the window will make everything better.

What happened? This is what researchers have called amygdala hijacking. When the emotional processor (the amygdala) kicks into high gear, the logic center processors (neocortex) get almost turned off and blocked. Adrenaline, hormone levels, and blood pressure rise, and our memories become less efficient. We begin to lose the ability to communicate effectively, and we turn to a form of autopilot to make decisions.

A group of researchers from Case Western Reserve University performed some tests to see if this is true. They recruited 45 college students and asked them to spend 10 minutes inside an MRI machine five times. The researchers presented them with a random set of 20 written and 20 video problems that required them to think about how others might feel. Then they received 20 written and 20 video problems that required physics to solve. After each question, they had to answer yes or no within 7 seconds. They were given 27-second rest periods in between, as well as variable delays lasting from 1 to 5 seconds between trials.

The findings were amazing. When the students were asked to answer questions and solve problems that triggered empathy, brain regions associated with analysis deactivated, and social regions of the brain activated. When the subjects solved problems and answered questions dealing with physics and logic, brain regions linked to empathy deactivated, and the analytical network activated. When the students had downtime lying on the table with no questions being asked, both regions of the brain were activated, allowing them to access both the analytic and moral/social regions of their brains.

What does this mean for the social engineer? Triggering, or hijacking, the emotional, empathetic, or social regions of the brain can shut down the person's ability to think logically.

Scam artists have known this (even without all the science) forever. This is why they use natural disasters, dying children, sickness, and other emotional triggers to part victims from their money. It works. When you find a story line that triggers that empathetic response, the person stops reasoning and starts handing out money.

Social engineers are no different. There are many accounts of social engineers using sadness, fear, and other emotional triggers to scam information, actions, or money from their targets.

Recall the example in Chapter 5 in which my goal was to infiltrate an organization using a USB key containing non-malicious malware. Recall that my pretext was to dress in a suit, walk into the company holding resumes that were wet with coffee, and ask the receptionist if I could use my USB key to reprint my resume before my job interview. As I approached the receptionist's desk, what happened? The gatekeeper (the receptionist) processed the external stimuli:

- Who is this?
- What does he want?
- How will I respond?

These questions might have been going through her processing centers. I needed to hijack her processing centers and turn off her logic center. This is where my story came in. Because I displayed sadness and concern, her amygdala processed the external stimuli of my story and facial expressions, which triggered her empathy center. This shut down her logic center, causing her to process my request in only the social regions of her brain.

I've found a few more pieces of research that drastically affect a social engineer's ability to utilize amygdala hijacking, as described next.

Human See, Human Do

A group of researchers from Northwestern University and the University of Wales Bangor (Li, Zinbarg, Boehm, and Paller) joined forces and wrote a paper titled "Neural and Behavioral Evidence for Affective Priming from Unconsciously Perceived Emotional Facial Expressions and the Influences of Trait Anxiety."

As stated in the paper's abstract, "Affective judgments can often be influenced by emotional information people unconsciously perceive, but the neural mechanisms responsible for these effects and how they are modulated by individual differences in sensitivity to threat are unclear. Here we studied subliminal affective priming by recording brain potentials to surprise faces preceded by 30-msec [millisecond] happy or fearful prime faces." In essence, Li et al., wanted to see if the brain subconsciously recognizes nonverbal communications and then reacts, or allows decision-making ability to be affected by them.

First they set a baseline using research from Raichle and Gusnard (2001, 2005) that theorizes that humans have an automatic system that constantly surveys their environment for stimuli. In other words, the system looks for nonverbal feedback that triggers people's understanding of the world around them.

This can explain why we sometimes feel nervous, tense, or even afraid in situations that seem to present no clear reason for those feelings. Our brains' "radar" may be taking in the environment around us and notice someone nonverbally displaying anger, fear, or other negative emotions, and this triggers in us feelings that put us on alert.

The researchers decided to show the students faces displaying surprise because the emotion of surprise can result from either a positive or negative experience. The researchers "reasoned that ambiguous expressions of surprise might be sensitive to the influence of subliminal happy or fearful primes [images shown before the images of surprise]." The study contained 140 surprise faces from 70 different people, seven happy faces, and seven fear faces.

Li et al., placed the students in a dimly lit, sound-controlled chamber facing a screen and communicated with them over an intercom. Each student viewed 70 faces showing surprise. These faces were primed (preceded) by either a fearful expression or a happy expression for 30 milliseconds. The face display was randomized and changed for each student. The students were asked to rate the surprise face as "extremely positive," "moderately positive," "mildly positive," "mildly negative," "moderately negative," or "extremely negative."

As the paper states on page 101, "Affective priming was demonstrated by a significant difference in mean ratings for surprise faces preceded by fearful versus happy faces." In other words, Li et al saw a significant increase in the surprise face being rated as either positive or negative based on what kind of 30-millisecond prime face preceded the surprise face.

Although Dr. Paller gave the same caution that Dr. Ekman always gives, which is not to read too much into *why* a person feels a certain way, he stated, "The ability to detect microexpressions may allow an observer to be more empathetic and sense someone's true intentions and motivations."

Another piece of research, the "visual cliff" experiment described in Chapter 1, demonstrates that even from infancy, our nonverbal communications play a major role in our reactions to a given situation. For social engineers this is a vital point to understand—for the three reasons described in the next sections.

Reading Other People's Expressions

Learning to read other people's nonverbal communication can help you understand their true intentions and motivations. Learning to notice subtle or not-so-subtle displays can help you as a social engineer communicate more effectively.

To reiterate the caution, knowing how to read an emotion is a powerful tool. But it's important not to get too caught up in looking for every little sign to the point that you forget to listen actively. Listening to the person you are interacting with can create a powerful connection of rapport and trust.

Balance is required when utilizing these skills.

Your Own Emotional Content

Facial expressions and nonverbal communications can alter a person's ability to make decisions.

What happens when you are stressed or nervous? Your muscles get tense, you may start to sweat, and you can become unfocused. That tension shown on your face and body can create tension and nervousness in your target. Unless your pretext is showing fear or stress, displaying that emotion can be confusing to the target.

Just like a baby who waits for nonverbal approval to cross a "visual cliff," people we make requests of are looking for cues to trust us or not. Therefore, it is important to practice and gain control of that tension and nervousness so that we display the right emotional content.

The same goes if your pretext is nervousness or fear, like the story I told the receptionist about how I spilled coffee all over my resumes right before my job interview. If I displayed calm, cool confidence during this distressing story, this approach might not have worked, because my nonverbal communication would be incongruent with my verbal communication.

Nonverbal Social Proof

Besides noticing your target's nonverbals, it is just as important to get the feel of the room. What is the crowd feeling? Take notice if there seems to be a somber mood, or if there is laughter. Noticing the mood of the room can help you to set your emotional content to match.

One time I was on a flight that arrived so late that I had missed not just one connection but two. As the plane approached the airport, the pilot came over the intercom to tell us that lightning had struck the airport and the electricity was out in certain sections.

The lightning had knocked out not only the main power but also the backup power. As I walked into the terminal, the only light was coming from airport security's flashlights. The concourse was in mayhem. Passengers were yelling at the employees, furious about missed flights and delays. I went to the gate I thought I was assigned to and found a long line of very angry people.

What was happening was a classic example of *social proof*, or the idea that the crowd's mood can give us permission to act a way we normally wouldn't act or take an action we normally wouldn't take. Everyone was mad, the scene was tense, and it was affecting all those around. Granted, your pretexts usually won't take place in such a tense situation. The point is that emotional content sometimes affects not just one or two people, but an entire room.

Even if you encounter a secretary at a company who puts on a sincere smile, noticing tension in the room can help you temper your emotions to match the mood or display emotion more appropriately.

When you keep these points in mind, as a social engineer, you can influence a person's ability to make decisions. The goal of the social engineer is to create an environment where empathy is easy to display. As you have learned, empathy shuts down the brain's logic centers. When those logic centers are not all firing together, that's the time to make your requests. The best conclusion to this section is to quote legendary New York talk show host Joe Franklin: "The key to success is sincerity—once you can fake that, you've got it made!"

Using Amygdala Hijacking as a Social Engineer

After reading the last few pages you may be wondering what any of this has to do with social engineering. Remember, the goal of a social engineer, whether good or nefarious, is to get the person to take an action. Understanding how the brain makes decisions can greatly aid the social engineer to get someone to make the decision you want them to make.

Personally, I like to simplify all these complex scientific findings so I can understand them better. The basic equation for amygdala hijacking is: (Sensory Input > Empathy) + Logic Center Shut Down = Amygdala Hijack + Request Made.

In essence, this says if a request is made after triggering the empathy response from a person, the request is more likely to be honored. How can this be used?

Our brains are hardwired to mirror the emotional content we see from those around us, so it is logical to say that if the social engineer can show mild sadness signs, those signs will trigger empathy in the person they are dealing with. Once empathy is triggered, and if the social engineer's words and story create an emotional bond with those words, then rational and logic centers in the brain shut down momentarily. This leaves the full processing power of our brain focused on the emotional center, so as a decision is being made based on the request, what is reasonable goes out the window.

I was doing a phone elicitation test once for a company. The goal was to call a company and try to elicit information that they should not have provided.

On one particular set of calls I decided to pretext as a fellow employee of the company named Jim. I made a few calls as "Jim" and was very successful in obtaining information and facts that would help me create a security program for the company.

I wanted to step up my game and decided to call the tech support group as Jim and see if I could get them to give me "my" VPN credentials over the phone. The call started like this:

"Tech support; this is Sue Smith. How can I help you?"

"Hi, Sue, I am having an issue. I deleted my VPN credentials while doing an online virus scan and now I can't get back in. I have a report due. Can you help me?"

"Sure, can I have your name?"

"James, but you can call me Jim."

"Jim, what is your user ID?"

"Actually can I just give you my full name? I always forget a few digits."

"Sure."

"James Ballo."

"Jim? Jim Ballo? Wait, you didn't recognize me? Its Suzie."

The conversation had been underway for about 30 seconds to this point, but now I was presented with a situation in which Suzie knows Jim and I am not acting like I know her. Facial expressions won't work because I'm on the phone, so how did I tackle this?

First, I let out an audible sign of frustration; it was long and definitely sounded stressed. Then I followed up with:

"Ah, Suzie, I am so sorry. I am such a moron (self deprecation). Today has been pure hell. I have a cold, which is why my voice sounds different (empathy building), then I deleted my certs, then I got yelled at by some other security guy (more empathy) for using an online scanner without permission, plus I got a flat tire this morning...." (more empathy). Then I let out another huge sigh.

"Oh, Jim, I am so sorry, sounds like a terrible day. What can I do to help?"

"I need to get this report over to my boss, and you know what he is like, and I can't get on the VPN. Can you just give me my credentials again?" (The request.)

Within moments I was being given the credentials I asked for, but why?

The equation again states that if I build empathy and mix it with my request I can shut off the brain's logic centers and get a person to take an action solely based on how they feel about a situation.

In the case in which I posed as Jim, I was not in person so I had to build empathy with limited nonverbals (the sigh) then the words (the sob story) before I made my request. Once I knew that Suzie was empathizing with me, even after having to explain away the fact that I should have known her, I then made my request, which was honored.

This is powerful in the way it works, and if done right, there is not much anyone can do to combat it. The key is knowing how to build empathy to the proper degree before making the request, and that comes with practice.

Summary

A social engineer doesn't need to be a researcher or a neurologist or a psychologist, but a good social engineer will at least understand what makes people tick.

To recap, let me outline the simple equation that makes up amygdala hijacking: Supporting nonverbal + emotional content of empathy + make the proper request = amygdala hijacking.

To simplify, a social engineer wants to build emotional content—especially empathy or sadness. The best way to do that is to support your words with proper nonverbals of sadness and empathy. Once the person's amygdala is triggered, the logic centers will shut down and that is when the request is made. If the request is reasonable, it will be honored, despite the best logical response.

Researchers like Dr. Ekman and the ones mentioned in this chapter have spent their lives trying to understand how emotions affect people. Reading and applying their research can go a long way toward developing your ability to hijack the emotions of the people you deal with.

On the flip side, when security professionals work with their clients, and they know about this research, they can notice environments where emotional hijacking can easily happen. Then they can help plan mitigations or training to enhance awareness of these types of attacks.

Knowing how these things work can help the social engineering professional find vulnerabilities and develop training and patches to fix them.

The next chapter takes these principles and expands on a topic covered in my first book—elicitation. Instead of covering all the details of elicitation, I will focus specifically on those aspects that utilize elements of nonverbal communication.

8

The Nonverbal Side of Elicitation

Feelings are much like waves: we can't stop them from coming, but we can choose which ones to surf.

—Jonathan Martensson

define *elicitation* as the act of getting information from someone without asking for it directly. This doesn't mean you don't ask questions, and it doesn't mean you don't ask for information. Military and intel folks, living acronyms, often joke about "ASKINT"—Ask Intelligence: "If you ask them, they will tell you!" It's all about how you ask about or around the issue. It means you employ techniques to gather this information from people. I usually refer to the techniques in Robin Dreeke's book *It's Not All About "Me": The Top Ten Techniques for Building Quick Rapport with Anyone.* In that book, Dreeke outlines 10 principles for building rapport with anyone; these are the keys to elicitation:

- **Artificial time constraints**: Using simple phrases—such as "Can I ask you a *quick* question?" or "I have to leave in *five minutes*, can I ask you a *quick* question?"—leaves the subject feeling more friendly about talking with you.

- **Accommodating nonverbals**: If you're saying that you're worried or sad and you're showing fear or anger in your nonverbals, then the subject will feel that incongruence. They may not understand why, but the red flags go up, and they feel uneasy. It is important that our nonverbal displays match the story.

- **Slower rate of speech**: The faster we talk the more prone we are to error, the more we sound like we aren't sure of ourselves, and the easier it is for the subject to view us as shady.

- **Sympathy/assistance** themes: As mentioned, empathy and sadness are strong links between humans. Using a pretext story that involves the subject helping you out creates a bond quickly.

- **Ego suspension**: One of the hardest to do, but also one of the most powerful. Suspending your ego, and making others' views, wants, and needs more important that your own, makes people want to be friends with you and like you. Suspending or putting on hold your own ego elevates another person's ego.

- **Validation**: When compliments are tactfully done and not overdone, they can make a person release dopamine, a chemical in their brains that plays a major role in reward-motivated behavior. That reward is enough to create a strong bond between you and that person.

- **Ask how, when, why questions**: These types of questions are open ended, encourage the person to engage their brain, and think about how they feel. This is very rewarding if the answers are listened to attentively.

- **Quid pro quo**: Latin for "this for that." People feel uneasy if they do all the talking with no feedback; to help the people you are talking to not feel uneasy it is a great idea to throw in a few nuggets about your life every now and then. Caution: Do not let a few small fragments turn into you taking over the conversation.

- **Reciprocal altruism**: When you give a gift to someone they (psychologically) have a need to reciprocate. Even simple things like holding a door will lead to a reciprocal gift in return.

- **Manage expectations**: These principles work so amazingly well that many times you can get excited and try to get too much information, raising your subject's defenses. Manage what you expect to get and how many principles you apply at one time.

After rapport is established, people feel comfortable giving you information, and they normally do so willingly and without regret.

Although I won't cover all 10 principles, I feel it is important to define them. I can't do any better than the excellent work Dreeke did in his book. Figure 8-1 shows you these principles.

Each principle has important nonverbal communication aspects. Yet each step can use a little help from the principle of accommodating nonverbals.

When someone approaches you in person or online, a series of questions runs through your head:

- Who is this?
- What does he want?
- Is he a threat?
- How long will he be a part of my life?

Figure 8-1: Ten principles to build rapport

Each principle is displayed nonverbally in a certain way that either adds to or detracts from the message being portrayed. The following sections examine a few principles and discuss how nonverbal communications affect them.

Artificial Time Constraints

As I mentioned previously, one of the first questions that we ask internally when a stranger approaches us is, "How long will you be part of my life?" Even if we answer the other questions that may be internally asked, leaving this one unanswered can make the person feel uneasy.

To help answer this from the nonverbal point of view, we need to understand that how we look affects the subject's view of our request.

If I ask you for help with a problem, psychologically, where should my interest lie? Your first reaction might be "With me, because you're asking for *my* help." But that would be incorrect. I am focused on my problem, not on you. Humans are self-centered. I don't know you. I'm interested in getting *my* problem fixed. If my body language says I *am* interested in you, that intensity will make you feel uncomfortable and will make the engagement harder. Also consider that there's a difference between requesting help for just a moment and asking for help for a longer period of time.

Therefore, I suggest that you create an artificial time constraint while facing to the side or even away from the target. This gives the impression that your interest is not in the person you are talking to, but in your problem. Doing so also reassures the person that you won't take up too much of his or her time.

For example, I once approached a customer in a bookstore to ask for some advice. He had his young son with him. Walking up to the bookshelf they were looking at, I stood to the side of him with my body facing the bookshelf. I turned only my head toward the man and said, "I'm sorry to bother you, but can I get your help for about 5 seconds? I need to buy a book for my nephew. I think your son is about his age. I'm a complete moron about this stuff. What do kids that age like to read?" My "5-second" request turned into a 25-minute conversation in which I found out the man's full name, birthdate, employment history, and many other pertinent details. I was able to build rapport quickly and follow up with elicitation because my nonverbal mixed with an artificial time constraint put him at ease.

Sympathy/Assistance Themes

I often say the four most powerful words in any social engineer's language arsenal are "Can you help me?" This request triggers an automatic psychological response in the other person to determine if helping is safe, convenient, and something that he or she should do.

As discussed in Chapter 7, if the social engineer can trigger empathy in the target, the target's logic centers shut down. This creates an environment more conducive to honoring a request.

I can best illustrate nonverbal communication for the sympathy/assistance themes principle with a story that didn't even involve a social engineering gig. I was walking out of my local grocery store when, a few yards ahead of me, an older woman wheeling her cart reached into her purse to pull out her car keys. When she did, something fell out. As I got closer, I saw it was a little wad of money.

I picked it up and began following her. As I approached, she was loading her groceries into her trunk. She was maybe 5 feet tall. As my 6-foot-3 frame loomed over her, I tapped her on the shoulder and said, "Excuse me. You dropped this money."

Her surprise turned into fear; perhaps she only heard "Excuse me" and "money." She began screaming "I'm being mugged!"

Immediately a couple of guys ran toward me—a large man in a black leather jacket, chain wallet, and jeans holding a wad of money in front of a small, elderly woman.

What was my mistake? My approach. Instead of coming at her from the side or walking up slowly, I was thinking "I'm here to help her," and I offered assistance with inappropriate nonverbals.

When social engineers ask for assistance, we need to plan our body language and facial expressions carefully. We want to display an appropriate level of sadness. We should not have our chest puffed out, standing in a dominant stance, showing fear, anger, or even happiness. At the same time, we don't want to appear so dejected and sad while making our request that we make people nervous.

Recall my interaction in the bookstore. If I had approached my target with tears running down my cheeks, the man may have grabbed his son and fled.

Tempering our nonverbal displays to match the emotion that is appropriate with the request is an important part of moving toward elicitation using the sympathy/assistance themes principle.

Sometimes we can elicit help without even having to ask. In one engagement I walked into the lobby of an office building and stood in a corner as I prepared for my approach. I must have let out a loud sigh, because as one of the gatekeepers passed me, she stopped and asked, "Are you okay, Honey?"

Thinking fast, I answered, "No, actually. Thanks for asking." I began to turn away slowly as I lowered my shoulders.

"What's wrong?" she asked. "Can I help?"

"Well, unless you get me in to meet with the head of HR in the next 5 minutes, probably not." I sighed again. I told her I was supposed to meet with someone in HR whose name I had forgotten.

"You're probably meeting with Beth Smith. I can get you in. Just come with me."

"Beth! Yes, that is it! Thank you so much."

"Now stop being nervous. It will all be OK," she told me as she buzzed me through the locked doors.

With a little nervousness, a couple of sighs, and matching nonverbals, I was in the door and roaming the halls.

Ego Suspension

Ego suspension is arguably the single most important aspect of rapport building, because it tends to lead to elicitation. Ego suspension is one of the most powerful principles a social engineer can use.

People like to be around others who are humble, who can admit they are wrong, and who let others be themselves. All of this requires you to suspend your ego. Nonverbal communication goes along with ego suspension.

Look back at Figure 5-1, but don't read the caption. What does it make you think of? Definitely not humility! Next, go to Figure 5-20. Again, do you see humility? Someone you want to approach? Most likely not. How about Figure 4-10? Again, all of these are examples of body and facial language that do not ooze humility. When we feel confident, nervous, upset, or rejected, we may display nonverbal behavior that does not display humility.

Think of one person you consider to be humble—one person who, when he or she talks to you, makes you feel important and good.

I had a close friend named Brad Smith. Unfortunately he passed away recently, but those who knew him would say he was a tremendous example of ego suspension. One incident that I can relate to show you the power of ego suspension involves Brad.

I was at a conference running a social engineering competition. One of the security people told me that in the evening my contest room would be converted into a party room. Hearing this upset me because I had equipment, banners, and electronics in there, and it was supposed to be exclusively my room. I was really upset, even now as I type this story I can feel my blood pressure rising.

A few people on my team said things like "It's okay; we'll make it work." and "Wow, that stinks." None of them helped me calm down or think rationally, not that it was their job, but I felt myself getting more upset. When I was almost at full-blown amygdala hijacking stage, Brad walked in and saw the stress on my face.

He approached me and lightly touched my arm, looked me in the eye, and, with a soft voice and lower body posture (bringing down his shoulders but not hunching), said, "Hey, can I talk to you alone for a few seconds?"

"Brad, I'm not in the best of moods," I snapped, quickly feeling bad.

"I know," he replied. "I can see why. But could you spare just a few minutes for an old man who doesn't know much?"

Wow! The light touch, soft voice, and non-condescending tone were all backed up by words spoken in a true form of ego suspension. We sat down and spent the next 20 minutes calming me down and helping my logic centers kick in so that I could fix the problem and move on.

That same day, an autistic young man attending the conference had a meltdown. People were becoming irritated. Brad approached the young man and—again with a light touch and a soft voice—said, "I don't think I know anything about you. Can you talk to me for a few minutes?" He sat with Brad for over an hour and calmly talked about his life. Brad helped him see how he could react better and deal with stress.

When we master ego suspension, like Brad did, making requests of others is easy, and getting those requests granted is even easier. Over the last year or two I have analyzed Brad and the interactions I had with him to see how any social engineer can harness this power.

Brad did a few key things that all play into the nonverbal portion of ego suspension:

- Lowering the voice
- Soft, nonsexual touches
- Mild gazes
- Lower body posture

These actions were followed by a request for help. How can you not want to help this kind of person? As you grant the request, a warm smile with a head tilt tells the person that you trust him, and that you appreciate his trust in return.

Ego suspension is powerful, and it works like magic to break down barriers and get people talking.

Ask How, When, and Why Questions

The last principle of building rapport to lead to elicitation I will consider from a nonverbal standpoint is the use of how, when, and why questions. Briefly, these types of questions are more powerful than where, what, and yes/no questions.

Suppose you ask someone either "Where did you go on vacation?" or "Why did you choose that area of Florida for your vacation?" Which question do you think is more likely to make someone open up? When you ask the second question, your subject has to formulate a response based on her emotions, likes, and dislikes, and the social engineer gets a glimpse of how she thinks. How, when, and why questions engage the person's brain, more than other types of questions.

Nonverbal language plays into these types of questions because how we hold ourselves while asking these questions makes the person feel either uncomfortable or trusting.

Look back at Figures 4-3 and 4-11. Which one shows Ben displaying body language that would put the target at ease?

In Figure 4-3, Ben's thumb display, facial expression, and square shoulders might make the target feel like Ben wasn't really interested in her answer, just the question.

In Figure 4-11, Ben is showing a ventral display and a nice facial expression that says he really is curious. Both the ventral display and the expression say he trusts the target and therefore can be trusted himself.

This is important to discuss because we naturally do these things when we ask questions. Sometimes during an engagement, though, we are focused on the goal or task at hand. When we focus on the goal, not the person, we begin to act unnaturally. Fear, tension, worry, irritation, or other emotions or feelings start to arise. When they do, our nonverbal language changes from "Trust me" to "Show caution."

These aspects of elicitation and rapport building are essential, but many other skills can help. Throughout this book I've referred to Dr. Ekman's research into something called *conversational signals*. The next section discusses them at length.

Conversational Signals

As I mentioned in Chapter 6 when I discussed comfort versus discomfort, sometimes it is easier to first look for little clues and then try to reinforce what you found by looking deeper.

Seeing a sign of discomfort is generally easier for the untrained than seeing a microexpression that lasts for 1/25 of a second. Along these lines, Dr. Ekman wrote a chapter in the book *Human Ethology* in 1979. In Chapter 3 he wrote about eyebrows being used as conversational signals.

Before getting deeper into describing conversational signals, I need to take a step back to the Facial Action Coding System (FACS) program mentioned in the Introduction and the three action units (AUs) that relate to these conversational signals.

Action Unit 1: Inner Brow Raiser

One large muscle runs vertically from the top of the head to the eyebrows, covers almost the whole forehead, and raises the eyebrows. To use this muscle, pull up the inner portion of the eyebrows. This causes the eyebrows to form an oblique shape, and the skin in the center of the forehead wrinkles (only in the center—not across the whole forehead). Figure 8-2 shows Dr. Ekman performing this action.

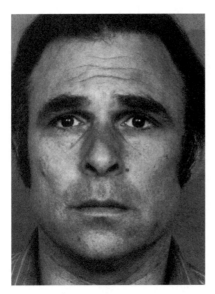

Figure 8-2: Action unit 1 from the FACS program

Action Unit 2: Outer Brow Raiser

The lateral part of the same muscle that helps create AU1 creates AU2. This action pulls up the eyebrows and adjacent skin. To create AU2, pull up the outer portion of the eyebrows. Doing so arches the eyebrows and stretches up the outer portion of the eye fold. Sometimes short wrinkles appear in the lateral portions of the eyebrows. Figure 8-3 shows this action unit.

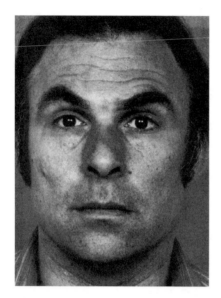

Figure 8-3: Action unit 2 from the FACS program

Action Unit 4: Brow Lowerer

Three strands of muscle run through the forehead and help control this action unit. Typically all three of these strands act together, although more of one strand than another may be involved in any of these actions. To create AU4, lower the eyebrows—the inner portion, the middle, or the whole brow. Contracting the muscles in this manner pushes down the eye fold cover, narrows the eye aperture, and pulls the eyebrows closer together. While pulling down the brows, do not wrinkle the nose. Figure 8-4 shows an example.

These details are pretty technical, but they are essential as a baseline for understanding the next section. As I talk about these conversational signals, I will refer to AU1, AU2, and AU4 used individually or in various combinations.

Figure 8-4: Action unit 4 from the FACS program

Conversational Signals of Emotions

Just as certain facial expressions indicate an emotion, you can look for signals during a conversation that can indicate an emotion that the person is feeling. The paper *Human Ethology* outlines the emotions I spoke about in Chapter 5 with these action units.

For instance, in surprise you notice both AUs 1 and 2. Both the inner and outer parts of the eyebrows are raised and arched, followed by the raising of the upper eyelids and the dropping of the jaw. In fear you see AUs 1 and 2, as well as 4 in combination with the raising of the upper eyelids, tightening of the lower lids, and stretching of the lips. In anger you notice AU4 with the brows coming down and together, and with a tightening of the lips and lower lids. In sadness you notice either AU1 or AUs 1 and 4, forming the brows in an inverted V. This is combined with the relaxation of the upper eyelids, slight raising of the cheeks, and depression of the chin.

AU4 can be seen in some expressions of both disgust and happiness, where the brows are lowered, though often more slightly in happiness.

All of this is closely connected to what I wrote about in Chapter 5. It is common for these eyebrow movements to occur without other facial expressions being involved. So what if you notice these AUs in the eyebrows without the accompanying facial movements?

Dr. Ekman has come up with some hypotheses that are labeled as conversational signals in regards to the meaning of eyebrow movement when not associated with other emotional facial movements.

I will outline some of the most commonly used conversational signals that Dr. Ekman found and show how important they are for the social engineer to recognize.

Breaking Down Conversational Signals

There are a few key factors to keep in mind when reading conversational signals. The research done by Dr. Ekman noted some differences between facial expressions and conversational signals. Mainly, conversational signals, unlike microexpressions, can change with culture.

In addition, a conversational signal is not something uncontrollable, like a microexpression. Most listeners are unaware of their own conversational signals. However, we can consciously choose to display conversational signals to "signal" to the other person to develop rapport, or to show that we are listening, in agreement, in disagreement, or some other message.

As I talk about this, try to make these combinations just in the eyebrows and see how you feel. Also picture in your mind what the next movement would be.

Batons

Similar to the hand batons mentioned in Chapter 3, these batons are used as an emphasis movement to accent a word. The most frequent baton found is the combination of AU1 and AU2, raising the eyebrows as high as they go, signifying surprise, questioning, or doubt. As a listener, a slight raise of the eyebrows can show a "pleasant" surprise—as "I'm impressed"—which can enhance rapport and encourage the listener to say more.

Another is the use of just AU4, which signifies cognitive load, confusion, or perplexity. Knowing that this eyebrow baton of AU4 can signify confusion, a social engineer would want to practice avoiding it when pretexting confidence. If we approach our target looking confused, we remove confidence.

On the other hand, the use of AUs 1 and 4 to display sadness by forming the brows in an inverted V (take a look Figure 5-11 for an example) can help the social engineer if the subject starts to show signs of reluctance to comply; while using only AU4 as a baton can show interest or concentration.

Underliner

To understand the underliner, think about underlining an important phrase in a magazine or book. As you do so, you cover many words—maybe even an entire sentence. The same is true of this conversational signal. A combination of AUs 1 and 2, or AU4 can be used, but imagine the difference in how while reading this. A person using an underliner may raise his voice or stretch out a word as it is spoken. What eyebrow movement or conversational signal do you see being used? The raised brow is what I see (AUs 1 and 2) as the words are being spoken, especially if the voice volume is getting higher and louder.

Punctuation

During a conversation you may want to punctuate certain words or phrases, maybe with an exclamation or even a question mark. This is often done using a conversational signal in the forehead.

AUs 1 and 2, or 4 can be in play in this conversational signal, but they are employed very differently. Whereas AUs 1 and 2 would be used as an exclamation, AU 4 is used to punctuate the seriousness of the words, the importance of what is being spoken, or the difficulty of what is being described. All of these signals punctuate the words as they are being spoken.

Question Mark

Maybe during a conversation you want to accentuate a question you have, or relay to your conversation partner that you doubt something that was said, or even more seriously are perplexed by something that was said.

AUs 1 and 2 are employed here, as you would imagine. These brow raises are used when people ask questions and also when they are unsure during an answer. If someone is perplexed during a conversation, she employs AU4 to lower her brows reflecting cognitive load.

Word Search

When you have trouble thinking of a word you want to say, what conversational signal is being used?

AU4. The eyebrows come together in the middle, displaying cognitive load (thinking), and you may even snap your fingers to try to remember the word. When you finally recall it, your eyebrows relax.

Another use of AUs 1 and 2 is when someone looks up, searching for his word. His eyebrows are raised with the eyes in that search.

Nonverbal Conversational Signals

You might be thinking, "All the conversational signals employ AUs 1, 2, or 4. What's so special about that?" Good question. When we see these being employed during a conversation, it should be easy to determine what they mean, right?

Imagine that you are listening to someone tell a story. During one section he employs AU4 bringing his brows down and together, his finger is outstretched, and his voice lowers. What's happening at this point? He's telling a serious, ominous, or negative part of the story.

This is easy to see when words are involved. Dr. Ekman's research found implications for the social engineer on the flip side of this scenario: when conversational signals occur without speech.

This is an important topic because understanding what someone may be conveying without speaking can enhance your ability to communicate and influence the subject. Remember, the following conversational signals are employed with no words being spoken.

- **Disbelief**: If someone employs AUs 1 and 2 while pulling down the corners of the lips, relaxing the upper eyelids, pushing up the lower lip, and rocking the head from side to side, this signifies disbelief.

- **Mock astonishment**: Combining AUs 1 and 2 with raised upper eyelids and an open mouth is commonly seen when someone is astonished.

- **Affirmation and negation**: This is an interesting one because its meaning differs depending on the culture in which it is displayed. In the West we see a head tilted back with a quick flash of AUs 1 and 2 as an affirmation. Yet among Greeks and Turks this is a negative, not an affirmation.

- **Sophisticated skepticism**: In sophisticated skepticism, AU2 is utilized on only one side of the face. That eyebrow is raised, signifying that the person is skeptical. Dr. Ekman found no naturally occurring example of this; he saw it only when it was being done on purpose to show skepticism. Therefore, if you notice this display, it is deliberate, not genuine. Dr. Ekman points out examples in films from the 1930s and 1940s. I associate this signal with something we might see from Mr. Spock in *Star Trek*. PK notes that John Belushi often used a classic one-brow raise to show obvious intended skepticism. This is not to say that the person is trying to deceive you, but it is not a naturally occurring signal.

- **The head nod**: PK and Dr. Ekman also note the effect of the head nod as a simple but effective conversational signal. How many times do you notice someone nodding their head (vertically) in the affirmative while you are speaking? Most times, the listener is unaware of this signal. By consciously nodding their head while listening, the speaker will take note, and being rewarded by the approval, be more at ease, and more talkative—a great technique for both rapport building and elicitation.

- Lastly, **the head bobble**: PK told me a story of when he first traveled to Pakistan, he noted a common variation of the head nod that was unknown to him. The listener began nodding his head laterally—not in the negative display of turning the head side to side, but like trying to move his ears slightly to his shoulders. He later asked about this and learned that this is a very common conversational signal in South Asia to reflect that your message is being understood and processed as the head bobs side to side. He saw this same regional signal during a trip to India.

Conversational Signals as a Social Engineer

There is probably no better way to summarize this section than with what Dr. Ekman said on *page 202 of Human Ethology:*

The student of emotional expression needs to understand the conversational signals as well. These actions occur often and if they are not recognized will confuse the study of emotional expression. The student of conversation must understand the emotional expressions if he is to disentangle them from actions that are directly guided by conversational process.

I couldn't agree more. It is vitally important as a social engineer for you to understand these signals. These little clues can help you see if your subjects are getting the point, showing disbelief, or becoming bored. You can then adjust your approach, enhance your style, and communicate more efficiently when you see these signals.

Remember, you need to practice only three AUs: 1, 2, and 4. Make this your mantra for conversational signals: Eyebrows up, eyebrows down, nod to encourage. Practice these so that you understand how they feel and how they make you feel. Looking for these signals in others and recognizing them during conversation can help you decipher the emotions of the person you are speaking to.

Summary

Elicitation is the crux of the social engineer's job. As a social engineer, I talk a lot about how to utilize elicitation tactics, but this chapter took a new approach to elicitation skills—the nonverbal approach.

This chapter has combined the work of Dr. Ekman with that of great minds like Robin Dreeke and Dr. Robert Cialdini. I have blended that information with the experience and practice I have gained over many years. This creates a recipe for success in any elicitation venture, whether you are a social engineer or not.

You may converse with many people throughout the day. We don't often think of all the aspects involved in a conversation—where our eyebrows are, how our body is positioned, what our face and hands are doing. Yet our conversations go well, and we relay and receive information just fine. How, then, can you use this information?

This is another arrow in the social engineer's quiver. The more signs you can recognize, the easier it becomes for you to rid yourself of negative traits and enhance the ones that make conversation easier. In a world where we've been spending more time texting, emailing, and posting on social media, conversational quality has diminished.

A 2011 study titled "Americans and Text Messaging" (`http://pewinternet.org/Reports/2011/Cell-Phone-Texting-2011.aspx`.) by Aaron Smith states that 31 percent of Americans would rather receive a text message than carry on a face-to-face conversation. And this percentage probably is even higher today because of Facebook, Twitter, Snapchat, Instagram, and other social media. The art of conversation, along with elicitation, is more important than ever for the social engineer to understand. That is what makes this chapter so important.

How do we put all this together? This book contains much research and information on how nonverbals play a serious role in our everyday communications. How can you put everything to use? That is the topic of the last chapter.

IV Putting It All Together

9

Nonverbal Communication and the ~~Social Engineer~~ Human Being

It is not who I am underneath, but what I do that defines me.

—Bruce Wayne/Batman

When I planned this book, I came up with what I thought was an appropriate table of contents. That is what I presented to my publisher as my concept for this book. The end results are drastically different than what I planned. This happened because as this book was being written, new research came out, changes occurred to the existing research, and my experiences and understanding changed as well.

I am telling you this because it is one of the first valuable lessons I feel this book can teach a social engineer: Things change quickly, and we must be able to adapt. Adaptation is what keeps us alive. If humans didn't adapt, we would die off.

When I analyze the malicious side of social engineering, I frequently see this ability to adapt. The "bad guys" can pick up new skills, utilize new technology, and change as the times change. Yet sometimes, when I work with companies as a social engineering consultant, I see a strong unwillingness to change or adapt. I hear comments like "We've been doing things this way for years. Why change now?"

Why? Because the world is changing. Yes, there have always been scam artists and con men and thieves, but lately we have seen a global influx of a cold-hearted type of criminal.

One example is the increase in attacks on the elderly, regardless of the amount of money they have. Criminals pretext as relatives or government agencies with the goal of taking every last penny these people have. The night before I wrote this chapter, I was discussing this topic with a close friend. He told me that the mother of one of his friends had just been victimized by a scam artist. She was dying of cancer and had very little money, but the attacker still took her for all she was worth through one or two phone calls.

The lack of concern for our fellow man has increased over time. Mix that with the ease of spoofing email addresses, phone numbers, and Internet identities, and you have a breeding ground for anyone who wants to try malicious social engineering.

In our business and personal lives, we can use software and processes to protect ourselves from malware, viruses, and Trojans. We can buy better locks and alarm systems for our doors, and we can even hire companies to monitor our credit reports. Yet we have little to no defense against the malicious social engineer. When such a person gets you to wire him money or give him your credit card number, no system, tool, or software can stop that.

I am not saying that there is no hope and that the future is bleak. I am saying that the fix is not easy. That is why I wrote my first book and now this book: The fix is knowledge and then action.

As with most things in life, you first take in knowledge: how these attacks are performed, what methods are used, the indicators of an attack, what is being attacked.

After that, the knowledge needs to motivate you to take action. That action is where the safeguards are. Knowledge is the only real protection against human hackers or social engineers. If you can recognize the signs and understand what is being said or, even more importantly, what is *not* being said, you have a chance at defense.

In this final chapter I want to discuss this information from two different viewpoints. First, I will discuss how you can put these things into practice as a penetration tester, using these skills to enhance your talents in protecting your clients. Second, I want to discuss how to use this book as a defense mechanism. Maybe you are reading this book because you are part of an IT team, or you are a professor or teacher, or you are a parent or concerned citizen. How can you use the information in this book to enhance your communication skills and to decipher whether someone is being sneaky with you?

Applying This Information as a Professional Social Engineer

My five-day "Social Engineering for Penetration Testers" class uses the motto "Leave them feeling better for having met you." Our goal in the five days is to teach each student the skills to elicit personal details from someone without using manipulation tactics or making the subject feel bad. What is amazing to me are the results—not the information gathered, but the results with the students. I have had students tell me the class changed their life and taught them how to be a better husband, father, person. How is this possible? Social engineering basically means learning to be a good communicator. If you learn to be a good communicator, with a goal of leaving the people you meet and communicate with feeling better for having met you, the results can be life-altering.

But a different lesson in those five days sometimes doesn't hit the students until the very end: Malicious social engineers employ the very same tactics.

I once interviewed Dr. Paul Zak for my podcast on www.social-engineer .org (the interview can be found at www.social-engineer.org/ ep-044-do-you-trust-me/). Dr. Zak does research on oxytocin, a molecule released in our brains when we feel trust, bonding, and closeness. It's often related to breastfeeding, but Dr. Zak has found that all humans release it, often when they interact with those they love and trust.He told me a story from when he was a young man working at a gas station, and a couple of con men tricked him using a ruse called a "pigeon drop." One day a man came into the office with a small box he said he found in the restroom that contained what appeared to be expensive jewels.

Just as Paul was deciding what to do, the phone rang. The man on the other end frantically described how he had left behind some jewels at the gas station. Paul told the man that an honest patron, standing right there, had just turned them in. The ecstatic man on the phone said he wanted to give the finder a $200 reward. Paul hung up and told the finder that the owner of the jewels wanted to give him a reward when he arrived to pick up his box. The finder replied that he was on his way to a job interview and had to leave, but he offered a solution: He would split the reward with Paul. All Paul had to do was take $100 from the cash register and give it to the finder. Then, when the jewels' owner arrived, Paul could keep $100 for himself and put the other $100 back in the register.

Paul did give the finder the money, but the jewels' owner never showed up, so Paul was duped out of $100. How could someone be fooled by this particular con? According to Dr. Zak, "A con works not because the con man convinces you to trust him, but he convinces you that he first trusts you." When you feel trusted, your brain releases oxytocin, your emotions get involved, your amygdala may be hijacked, and logic centers go in the opposite direction.

This is a key point for the social engineer. When someone feels you trust him, he reciprocates with trust feelings. This is the valuable lesson that the security enthusiasts who attend my five-day class learn. They don't learn how to dupe, trick, or prove someone is stupid. They learn that people are more easily duped and duped for a longer period of time when the deception is carried out with kindness and trust.

After I wrote my first book, I received many requests for interviews. One of the early questions surprised me: "Aren't you afraid you're giving the bad guys more tools to use against us?" My answer was the same then as it is now: We can't defend properly without knowing how to attack. If the first time you get punched is your first real fight, it will most likely end badly for you. That is why people take lessons in how to fight and defend themselves. In those classes they do what is called *sparring*, in which two people actually hit each other to learn how to hit, how to take a hit, and how to defend against being hit.

That is what a penetration test is like—learning how to take, deliver, and defend against a hit. If you were preparing for a title bout, you wouldn't grab some 90-pound guy off the street to spar with. You would choose a sparring partner who had skill, size, strength, and experience. What kind of penetration testing sparring partner do you want? One who is in the ring for the first time, or one who knows how to fight properly and can prepare you for your title bout?

One quote I have heard that I am beginning to believe more and more is from McAfee's former VP of threat research, Dmitri Alperovitch. He said, "I am convinced that every company in every conceivable industry with significant size and valuable intellectual property and trade secrets has been compromised (or will be shortly), with the great majority of the victims rarely discovering the intrusion or its impact" (www.pcworld.com/article/237163/McAfee_Warns_of_Massive_5_Year_Hacking_Plot.html).

The bad guys aren't hitting up the local bookstore and going to the "how to be a bad guy" section. They learn on the job. Yet the good guys have few resources to help them learn the skills that will help them defend against attacks.

As a social engineering professional, I tell people to first practice these skills in the wild. For example, you can learn how to be a better conversationalist. Learn how to listen, how to use nonverbal communication to express emotion properly, and how to read others. As you do, you will see that you cannot shut off this instinct. It will start to open a new world for you.

The other day I finished writing Chapter 8. Because I had just reread Dr. Ekman's work, those pages were still fresh in my mind. As I spoke with friends, I couldn't help but see action units 1, 2, and 4 all over the place. I was picking up these signals with and without conversation, and doing so solidified that chapter even more for me.

To reiterate a point I made earlier in this book, "Perfect practice makes perfect." The more you use these skills with family, friends, coworkers, and strangers, the more they become a part of your personality. After that happens, you can move to the next part, which is using these skills as a social engineer.

This is probably one of the hardest uphill battles that professional social engineers face. I know from my discussions with some of the world's greatest, like Kevin Mitnick, Chris Nickerson, and Dave Kennedy, that we all have the same problem. Many companies do not see how important it is to test real social engineering vectors. They believe that a few easy-to-spot phishing emails and a couple of USB drops constitute a "social engineering test." You must help your customer see that the bad guys don't just send one or two emails and then give up, or drop a few USB keys in your parking lot and then leave. Attackers are focused and driven and don't give up easily. They don't go home at 5 p.m. and relax. They spend time profiling, gathering intel, and developing realistic attack vectors that work. How can a company expect anything less from its protection team?

When I was sitting with Dr. Ekman in his home, discussing the future of social engineering and nonverbal communication, I commented that it must be hard to catch him in a lie because of everything he knows about manipulating the face. But he replied that actually he is a terrible liar. However, over the decades he has practiced, tested himself, and taught himself to pick up on cues that can indicate that someone is lying. This practice has enabled him to work as a leader in his field since 1954 and write over a dozen books and publish over 100 articles on this topic. What does this mean for you and me? The same rules apply. We can utilize the research that took Dr. Ekman and other great minds decades to develop and work it into our everyday lives, becoming social engineering masters.

Using This Book to Defend

Let me return to my example about learning to fight. I once knew a guy who was a master swordsman. He was amazing with any blade. It took him about five years to get where he was, and then he spent the next five years perfecting the little things. When he started learning, he searched for just the right partner and teacher. Why? Because whomever he chose would be swinging very sharp objects at his head and body. Along with looking for someone who had knowledge and talent, my friend told me that another of the key factors he looked for was experience. Choosing someone with a proven track record meant that he could shorten the learning curve and enhance his abilities more quickly.

This is why I worked for over two years to develop close relationships with Dr. Ekman and Paul Kelly before I considered writing this book. I wanted to make sure I had a couple of "grand masters" on my side to help me reduce some of the learning curve for both you and me. Partnering with the masters of this science means that you and I benefit from the expertise, talent, knowledge, and, most of all, experience of the greatest minds in this area of research.

This helps you because keeping up on all the tactics and methods used by scam artists is time-consuming. I spend many hours every week reading news stories and reports about the latest attacks and the newest research into how humans work. But that is my job—to be the best so that I can protect my clients. You probably have a job, a family, and a life outside security. This book is designed to help you find easy ways to practice and implement the skills I've presented.

Let me step away from security for a moment and focus on communicating with other people. Whether you are communicating with your kids, your spouse, your boss, your students, people you meet in the store or on the street, people at your place of worship, or people you meet by chance, using these skills to become a better communicator will change how you send and receive information.

Being able to understand what someone is truly saying without words can help you alter your style to get your message across more proficiently. If you utilize that skill to create security measures, you will not only communicate better but also notice the signs of when someone is not communicating with clear intent.

After you are armed with this knowledge, insert this knowledge into your security awareness programs. Help the people you work with see how these skills are used by malicious social engineers. Teach them to be critical thinkers, and show them how just thinking through requests made can make a huge difference.

Becoming a Critical Thinker

In the summer of 2012, I read a newspaper article that said the Republican Party in Texas, as part of its official platform, opposed the teaching of critical-thinking skills in the public schools. I was amazed that anyone would want to forbid teachers from instilling in our kids one of the most fundamental skills they could gain.

Many times people equate critical thinking with rebellion, or with a lack of faith, or with questioning everything just for the sake of questioning. I do none of those things. I have strong faith. Although I am a typical "hacker" in the sense that I like to circumvent the norm and figure out how things work, I am not truly rebellious. I enjoy law and order.

My definition of critical thinking means teaching yourself, your family, your employees, and your clients not to accept everything at face value. Do not blindly accept the fact that I am your waste management representative, OSHA inspector, Joe from IT, or the assistant to the company vice president. Question such a fact if it doesn't sound right, if you haven't heard it before, or if you are uncertain why someone is calling you and asking you a question.

Critical thinking takes time and sometimes can be risky. For example, I once worked with a company that used a lot of call centers for support. They had a policy that after a support representative had spent over two minutes on the phone with a customer, his or her hourly pay rate decreased during the time that the call continued. Knowing this, during an audit, all I had to do was call them and keep the conversation going for this amount of time. The rep started getting tense, wanting to end my call so that he could maintain his pay rate. At that point I started to make my requests for sensitive information. Because of the stress on the rep, he stopped thinking critically and started answering whatever question I posed. This was especially true when I would say something like "I don't want to keep you any longer. Just let me ask you this one last question." This comment gave the rep some hope that the call would end soon. Then I would ask questions like, "Listen, I am starting a small business and it is important that I try to be like the big boys. There are so many choices for trash removal—who do you use?" Or maybe another question like, "I am just setting up my office and I don't know what kind of operating systems and other software to run. What operating system do you use? What browser?"

Waiting until just before time ends on their call means that the person is no longer thinking about logical reasoning but focusing on their pay scale and therefore making bad decisions about what information to give out.

Encouraging critical thinking skills within a company would reward employees for protecting company assets by questioning, thinking, and stopping an attack. Instead, companies often reward the very behavior they do not want the employee to carry out.

To assist my clients with critical-thinking skills, I've developed what I call Critical Thinking Scripts (CTSs). These aren't written-out, word-for-word conversations they should have, but a series of thoughts that will help them develop habits that keep them secure. For example, one script I wrote describes steps to follow when you use an ATM:

1. Look at your surroundings, and make sure they appear safe.
2. Don't take out your card until you're in front of the machine.
3. Before inserting your card, wiggle the card slot to ensure that it is part of the machine and is not a skimmer (a card reader installed by a hacker).
4. Look for any protruding pieces or weird-looking parts, which could indicate a skimmer (a small device that fits over the card slot and steals your data and passwords).
5. Insert your card, and shield the keypad while you enter your PIN.
6. Take your money, card, and receipt, leaving nothing behind.
7. Put everything in your wallet before leaving.

This simple CTS can protect you from being mugged or victimized by a skimmer. You should help your employees or clients develop CTSs for situations such as these:

- What should I do if I suspect that an email is a phish?
- What should I do if I just clicked a link in an email that might be a phish?
- What should I do if I suspect that a phone call is a phish?
- What should I do if I suspect that this person doesn't belong here?
- What should I do if I just answered questions that maybe I shouldn't have?

You face a challenge if the company's response to an employee's falling prey to a phish or other attack is punitive. If that's the case, it's very unlikely that employees will want to openly discuss security concerns and practices. But management needs to realize that being tricked by a malicious social engineer doesn't make someone weak or stupid—it makes him or her human. Employees must be helped to mitigate and fix problems so that the aftereffects can be minimized. The best way to do that is to give them a department or person they can report security incidents to without fear of being disciplined. You may also consider offering them extra training.

Summary

Writing this book was a learning experience. Having the opportunity to work closely with Dr. Ekman and Paul Kelly changed how I use and view nonverbal behavior. The more studying, reading, writing, and comparing I did, the more I started to see these signs in everyday conversations. This helped me communicate better, have richer conversations, understand the emotional content of those I was dealing with, and, of course, be more secure. No one magic technique described in this book can transform you into a human lie detector or mind reader. But combining the skills described in this book can give you amazing abilities to understand what someone is truly saying, even without words.

As you practice these skills, remember what Dr. Ekman told me when I started down this path with him a few years ago: "Just because you can see what someone is feeling doesn't mean you know *why* he is feeling that way." Learn to use the emotions you see to focus your elicitation efforts. Learn to notice the subtle things that point to a baseline. These things will give you a leg up in any communication—as a professional social engineer or not.

You may reach out to me if you want to discuss or even debate the points in this book. My website is `www.social-engineer.com`. There you will find ways to communicate with me directly. I am always open to a discussion.

Thank you for spending some of your valuable time with me in the pages of this book. I hope you have found a few gems of information you can use in your life. I know I have through my journey.

As a final point, please remember my motto: Leave people feeling better for having met you. Some people try to accomplish their goals through embarrassment and humiliation. Some try to teach a lesson using fear and ridicule. But I learn better if I'm taught with humility, kindness, and encouragement. I learn better from critical thinking. Take the time to see the problem from someone else's eyes, whether he is a child or just acting like one. Take time to understand his emotions whether they make sense or not, and whether they are rational or not. I guarantee that when you do, a new world will open to you. You will be able to unmask not just social engineers, but also any human who stands before you.

Index